# SOCIALISM AND THE EMERGENCE OF THE WELFARE STATE

## A CONCISE HISTORY

ALLAN MITCHELL

Printed in the United States of America.

ISBN: 978-1-4669-6293-4 (sc)
ISBN: 978-1-4669-6295-8 (hc)
ISBN: 978-1-4669-6294-1 (e)

Library of Congress Control Number: 2012918823

*Trafford rev. 10/09/2012*

 www.trafford.com

North America & international
toll-free: 1 888 232 4444 (USA & Canada)
phone: 250 383 6864 ♦ fax: 812 355 4082

# CONTENTS

Preface                              vii

Chapter 1  Marx                        1

Chapter 2  Germany                     7

Chapter 3  France                     24

Chapter 4  Britain                    41

Chapter 5  Sweden                     49

Chapter 6  United States              56

Conclusion                            67

Index                                 75

# PREFACE

It is not coincidental that this small volume was conceived during the American presidential electoral campaign of 2012. How many times in that year did we hear some partisan orator declaim that Barack Obama had every intention of leading the United States down the disastrous path of European socialism in order to create a welfare state? There are two obvious problems with such an assertion. First, Europe is a vast and variegated society in which each nation has a long and distinctive history. Surely the USA is not the only country that can claim "exceptionalism." Vaguely grouping all European states together, while ignoring their essential political and social differences, will certainly not increase our understanding of this complex issue. Second, accordingly, the development of social democracy necessarily assumed various and often quite dissimilar forms in the several nations of Europe. It would doubtless be more accurate to speak of European socialisms, and that requires a historical survey.

It is not necessary to tune in to cable television news programs to hear charges about President Obama's alleged socialist plot. Just down the hill from my home near Boulder, Colorado, stands a venerable restaurant called the Greenbriar. It boasts a wood-paneled bar nearly a century old, the closest thing to a British pub (minus the dartboard) that one could imagine. For years a small crowd of locals—sometimes just two or three, sometimes a dozen or more—gathers there on Thursday evenings. They are a diverse group in terms of education, occupation, and political views. This has been my window on the world, and through it I see a broad spectrum of current American public opinion, including the repeated contention that our nation is being coaxed down the road to a European-style welfare state. There is genuine concern and sincerity in those exclamations, but also a dollop of ignorance. As the lone scholar of European history in the gathering, I have felt an obligation to offer a coherent response. Generously, the anti-Obamists have offered to give me a chance and to read the result, which is this book, dedicated to them.

The scholarly studies directly related or relevant to the theme of socialism and social welfare can literally be counted by the thousands. Of course a single author could not conceivably read all of them in a lifetime. One is forced to choose. In the course of composing this synthetic overview of the subject, I have attempted to do so as judiciously as possible, and it seems altogether proper to indicate here the names of some historians whose work has been particularly valuable in the preparation of this volume. It has been my honor to become personally acquainted with most of them and to benefit from their insights: Peter Baldwin, Volker Berghahn, François Caron, Paul Dutton, François Ewald, Henri Hatzfeld, Hans-Gerhard Haupt, Peter Hennock, Colin Jones,

Jürgen Kocka, Gerhard A. Ritter, Christoph Sachsse, Timothy Smith, Florian Tennstedt, Hans-Ulrich Wehler. Obviously this list could be much longer, but my special thanks are due to those mentioned.

# Chapter One

## MARX

In the beginning was Karl Marx. No other writer of nineteenth-century Europe had remotely as much influence as he. The time and place of his birth were crucial to that importance. Marx was born in the town of Trier (Trèves in French) on the Moselle River only a few miles from the intersection of Germany and France with Luxemburg. It also happens that Trier stood on the border between the Germanic and Roman worlds that had collided there centuries ago. Hence Trier is a historic crossing in the heart of Europe. As for the timing, Marx was born in 1818 near the climax of the first industrial revolution in Britain and at the post-Napoleonic beginning of a second industrial wave of growth that swept over western continental Europe as the nineteenth century unfolded. As a boy, therefore, Marx grew up in a largely rural setting that was soon to be transformed by the innovative force of new commerce and industry. For the first time, everything that we think of as "modern"—meaning a growing population, advancing technological innovation, a burgeoning factory system, mass transportation, an increasingly numerous working class, and much more—was putting in an appearance amid great confusion and conflict. It was Marx's self-appointed task to bring all this remarkable unprecedented activity into focus.

His earliest writings, starting about 1840, tended to get lost in the shuffle. More than a century later they were scooped up by scholars eager to show that Marx was really a humanist, an existentialist, or whatever. But what those first essays actually revealed was that Marx began as a thoroughly convinced Hegelian. It was, after all, Hegel's theoretical *Weltanschauung* that preoccupied Marx during his initial philosophical studies at the university in Berlin. In 1846 he attempted to pull his own thoughts together in a treatise entitled *The German Ideology*. The lingering traces of Hegelianism were evident enough, but one crucial sentence set Marx apart from his master: "Here we do not descend from heaven to earth, but we ascend from earth to heaven." If taken to its ultimate conclusion, this newly found conviction meant that Marx would no longer begin with some abstract notion seeking to realize itself in history, but he would take a more positivistic approach by deducing abstractions from historical facts. Of course, he never quite succeeded in making a total transition to that objective, and his writings remained marked by the titanic clash of great concepts.

Let it be briefly added here that Marx well understood Hegel. A single illustration will serve to underscore that assertion: the most fundamental Hegelian proposition of the dialectic. This conception has often been presented as a kind of ethereal tennis match. First an idea (the thesis) is advanced, which is then met by an opposing idea (the antithesis). The resolution of their clash is another idea (the synthesis) that becomes a new thesis, and so on. But the fallacy of this analogy is exposed by asking a simple question: in a tennis tournament, where does the opponent come from? Of course the answer is: from another bracket. Not, however, in Hegel's dialectic. For him the antithesis must be sought within the original thesis. Thus the dialectical method is a repeated process of self-contradiction and intellectual refinement. Marx well comprehended this distinction, and to suit his purposes he transposed it into historical terms with his signature assertion that the capitalist bourgeoisie plants the seeds of its own destruction by creating within the industrial system a revolutionary proletariat.

Such was the setting for the most notorious of Marxian texts, *The Communist Manifesto*, written with his friend Friedrich Engels in 1848. The chaotic insurrectionary events of that year begged for a coherent interpretation, which Marx and Engels intended to supply. More than that, they hoped to move the historical process along with a provocative theory that the proletariat—Europe's emerging industrial working class—was now rising to overthrow the currently prevailing dominance of the bourgeoisie, that despicable exploitative class of entrepreneurs. The state, invariably an instrument of the ruling class, would doubtless attempt to provide soldiers and arms to suppress this immense uprising of workers, but ultimately the revolution was bound to succeed in overthrowing the existing social order and establishing a classless society.

There, as succinctly as possible, was the gist of Marx's conception. When things did not turn out just as he had wished and predicted, after being exiled from Germany and taking up residence in London, Marx devoted his mature years to composing a massive tome of macroeconomic theory, *Kapital,* which sought to explain how the inexorable march of history would nonetheless cause the inevitable collapse of the capitalist system and bring proletariat the to power. His hopes for that outcome in his own lifetime were briefly sparked by the Paris Commune in 1871, but its demise left Marx to claim that this one more failure was actually the harbinger of a new society that would be created by a successful world revolution. Famously, that cry was echoed near the end of the First World War by Lenin, who proclaimed the Bolshevik Revolution to be the dawning fulfillment of Marx's dream.

Compressed here to its essentials, that is the story of Karl Marx. How is it to be judged? The timing of revolutionary success aside, he was demonstrably mistaken about any number of matters. Three stand out. First, Marx was convinced that the great revolution would necessarily occur in the industrially most advanced countries, that is, in those where capitalism was most fully developed. Surely he was dead wrong about that. No more inhospitable soil for the spores of revolution could be imagined than that of the Great Britain where Marx took up residence after 1848. While living there for more than three decades in the London working-class district of Soho, he existed in a Germanic bubble with rosy memories of the past, great expectations for the future, but little appreciation of the immediate present at his door. English workers of the late nineteenth century were scarcely given to Marx's brand of insurrectionary theory, and it required a large dose of self-deception on his part to think otherwise.

Second, Marx falsely assumed that the state was destined to play but a single role: by definition, it must always and only be the instrument of the ruling class. Government power would therefore be wielded everywhere to favor the wealthy few at the expense of the less fortunate many. The form of government might vary, but its function would nevertheless be immutable: to buttress the haves against the have-nots. Hence the sole recourse was a revolution to overthrow the state. Marx expressed this conviction in the starkest terms, verging on caricature. The English translation of *Kapital* repeatedly refers to the capitalist as "Mr. Moneybags," whereas workers are reduced to the status of "wage slaves." In these drastic terms we detect more of the Hegelian dialectic than of factual analysis. Too often, in his later writings, Marx continued to descend from heaven to earth.

Third, Marx assumed that the proletariat had no fatherland. The Marxist cause predicated the international solidarity of workers everywhere, who would come to realize the communality of class rather than of country. Yet if there was one obvious and invariable emotion that seized nineteenth-century Europe, it was nationalism. At the outset of the First World War patriotic enthusiasm spilled spontaneously into the streets of every capital on the Continent. Workers willingly became soldiers. They fought and died for their *patrie*, regardless of class or social condition.

All of that said, Karl Marx was nonetheless profoundly correct in his most fundamental insight, the implications of which were amply spelled out in *Kapital*. Namely, it lies in the essence of capitalism that a relatively few individuals must be rich and that most persons must lead a more modest existence, many of them not far removed from the edge of poverty. In short, by its nature the capitalist system dictates that its common folk should perpetually serve their more fortuned overlords. Otherwise capitalism, the embodiment of social inequality, could not exist and would not function.

This concise balance sheet enables us to explore, define, and evaluate what socialism means. In substance, social democracy was at once a positive response to Marx's sprawling scenario and an attempt to mitigate its more negative consequences. The socialist vision was that the state might properly intervene to ameliorate the condition of the working class by fostering a redistribution of wealth through social benefits. Workers could organize and assert their claim to a fair share of capitalism's proceeds. Socialism was therefore reformist rather than revolutionary. But it also proved to be an extraordinarily diverse and complex movement that assumed different forms and met various fates in the individual European nations as well as in the United States. It is only by unraveling the multiple strands of this history that the origin and evolution of socialism can be brought clearly into view.

# Chapter Two

# GERMANY

To analyze the various forms that socialism assumed in the nineteenth century, it is appropriate to begin with Germany—and not merely because it was the homeland of Karl Marx. The early emergence of socialism there as a conspicuous actor on the world stage coincided with the second industrial revolution, when Germany took the lead in key industries such as dyestuffs, chemicals, electricity, and automobiles. This circumstance gave German socialism a special urgency, and it was there that the different versions of socialist doctrine were most clearly articulated.

But that is to get far ahead of the story, which properly begins deep in the background of Prussia's development after the Napoleonic wars. Under terms of the Vienna peace settlement of 1815, Prussia stretched across all of northern Germany from Silesia to the Rhineland, from Breslau to Cologne. As the first half of the nineteenth century unfolded, five major factors (not confined to Prussia alone) became observable:

1) *Rapid population growth.* Between the battle of Waterloo and the beginning of the Franco-Prussian War in 1870 the population of Prussia increased by more than 70 percent.

2) *Urbanization.* At least 80 percent of Prussians could be classified as rural as this period began, whereas inner migration from countryside to city decisively tipped the balance to urban areas by inception of the German Kaiserreich in 1871.

3) *Improved transportation.* Above all, the introduction of railways, starting in the 1830s, facilitated the movement of goods and people on an unprecedented and ever expanding scale.

4) *Thriving economy.* On the European continent, this proved to be the first age of large factories where uncounted thousands of workers became employed in the manufacturing process and when fabled names like Krupp, Borsig, and Siemens rose to prominence.

5) *State participation.* Ever since the days of Frederick the Great in the eighteenth century the Prussian monarchy had enjoyed a largely positive image among its underlings, although the state's direct contribution to the evolution of social policy remained meager.

Taken together, these five basic factors explain the dynamics of transition and innovation that were to make Germany into the industrial giant it became by the late nineteenth century. That was the good news. The bad news was that this remarkable transformation was accompanied by social dislocation, rampant unemployment, and widespread poverty. Inevitably, also, the concentration of labor and machines in the process of industrialization meant an alarming increase in the number of industrial accidents. These problems came to stay, and by mid-century they had to be faced.

But how? The abortive revolution of 1848 obviously indicated that trouble was at hand and that the measures of relief heretofore undertaken by government agencies and charitable institutions were inadequate. The first instance of Prussian social legislation in 1839 was primitive at best, amounting to a kind of poor law that brought little aid to the indigent and injured. If it can be said that there was a dominant social philosophy at stake, it was a notion of liberalism that promoted self-help, individual liberty, limited state intervention, and free commerce. In the late 1840s Prussia adopted a so-called *Gewerbeordnung* that specified some regulations for factory workers. These initial measures may be seen as a mincing effort to establish a state social policy. Yet their institutional expression was known as the *Hilfskasse*, that is, a voluntary form of social insurance that conformed tightly with the liberal principle of self-help. A prime example was the Elberfeld system of social assistance, named after a German textile center where it originated (and where, incidentally, Friedrich Engels owned a factory).

Such was the setting for the General German Workers' Association, founded by Ferdinand Lassalle in 1863, the first socialist labor organization of note on Prussian soil, which was the godfather of a growing trade union movement as the century progressed. Lassalle was persuaded that state-help needed to be substituted for self-help, and to that end he "negotiated" with the Prussian prime minister Otto von Bismarck in the following year. A decidedly one-sided conversation it was, as Bismarck remarked, since Lassalle had really nothing to offer him in return. Nonetheless, in the 1860s the first signs of an economic boom were becoming apparent, and the workers' cause was stirring. In 1866 Wilhelm Liebknecht and August Bebel formed a People's Party in Saxony, and three years later, in the midst of a strike wave, they declared the creation of a German Social Democratic Party (SPD) in the city of Eisenach. In that same year, 1869, a new set of labor regulations was promulgated by the North German Confederation (an expanded version of Prussia), which sought to assuage the nascent labor movement but which still depended on the voluntary *Hilfskasse*, although it asserted the right of the state to intervene when necessary in economic and social affairs—just as Bismarck wished. There matters stood as Germany entered the victorious war with France in 1870.

The birth of the German Kaiserreich, famously proclaimed in the Hall of Mirrors at Versailles in January 1871, was immediately followed by the riotous aftermath of the Paris Commune. By releasing French prisoners of war with their weapons, Bismarck saw to it that the Commune was repressed, but the bogeyman of rebellious workers in revolt was to live on. The "red menace" had arrived, personified in imperial Germany by the merger of Lassalle's Workers' Association with the SPD in 1875. From its inception as a unified political organization, German socialism displayed three marked characteristics. First, there was a close alliance between the party and the trade unions; and, if anything, the unions tended to pull the party toward moderation. Second, within the entire socialist movement there was a notable contrast between a sometimes radical rhetoric and steady centrist reform actions. Third, socialist expectations were generally high that political agitation could ultimately succeed in attaining a significant redistribution of national wealth in favor of the lower classes. German social democracy, in short, was ambitious in the pursuit of a more egalitarian society.

Political allies in the 1870s, Bismarck and the German liberals had other notions. Their strategy was to firm up state control against any potential insurgency, to avoid alienating the proletariat by making it beholden to the existing order, and thereby to build the new Reich on a solid foundation of state-sponsored socialism. Two tactics would serve this end: to denounce the agitation stirred by the Paris Commune, and to pursue a policy of carrot-and-stick by combining liberal reforms (that did little to alter social inequality) with repressive measures. As for the latter, after two failed attempt on the Kaiser's life—falsely blamed by Bismarck on the socialists—the infamous anti-socialist laws were passed by the Reichstag in 1878 and remained in effect until 1890, the end of the Bismarck era. But despite the ban on party organizations, unions, demonstrations, and publications, the socialist movement continued to grow. Whereas August Bebel was the lone SPD deputy in the 1871 national parliament, the party boasted twelve delegates by 1877. Trade unions grew apace, and the popular vote for the SPD more than trebled, reaching 38 percent in Saxony, 39.2 percent in Berlin, and 40 percent in Hamburg. These trends persisted: by 1890 the SPD would garner nearly a million and a half votes and thirty-five seats in the Reichstag. And the German trade union membership subsequently ballooned to two and a half million, Europe's largest, by 1914.

The atmosphere of the 1880s was quite different from the preceding decade in more than one respect. For one thing, the economic slump that had struck in 1873 was dissipating. For another, Bismarck ended his alliance with the National Liberal Party and took a turn to state protectionism, away from liberal free trade policy. The constant, however, was carrot-and-stick, ever more emphatically stressed by the Chancellor. It would be a mistake to exaggerate this circumstance by crediting Bismarck alone with the creation of a state socialism. Still, the legislation of the 1880s would surely not have taken shape without his intervention, and it did lay the groundwork for a structure of social welfare legislation that became a model for the rest of Europe. Few historical subjects have been so extensively studied, so there is no need to belabor the details here. The major enactments may be swiftly listed: national sickness insurance in 1883, accident insurance in 1884, plus old-age pensions and disability insurance in 1889. Several qualifications should be registered. The actual benefits of these programs were initially very modest. They were restricted principally to industrial employees and factory workers with little effect on the rural population. They were usually administered by and largely confined to municipalities. And, contrary to Bismarck's wishes for a more unified system, they remained separate operations with varying degrees of success. Willy-nilly, before 1914, probably a quarter of German citizens received some direct insurance compensation, and, by including their families, perhaps half were thus to some extent covered.

One feature of Bismarckian social insurance needs to be emphasized: in the midst of all this complexity hovered a central principle of obligation. The voluntarist ethic that had prevailed before 1870 gradually gave way to a compulsory state-sponsored social security system—or, as the Germans chose to put it, the *Hilfskasse* was replaced by the *Zwangskasse*. In essence, it was a deal that socialists, with few exceptions, could not refuse. But it came at a cost of acknowledging the state's prerogative to supervise and regulate the labor market. True, Bismarck did not obtain all that he wanted: a centralized state-dominated social insurance scheme financed solely through taxation and a national tobacco monopoly. Nor did he finally succeed in imposing a "right to work" that would curtail labor strikes. Yet he did design the framework of a social security network that exists to this day. As for German social democracy, most of its adherents bowed to the practical necessities of a reformist centrism, comforted by the thought that they were thereby seeking to establish a "third way," in effect a safe passage between unfettered capitalism and radical communism. At first skeptical, in sum, the Social Democratic Party slowly came around to a positive view of the Reich and its social legislation.

In the quarter century before the First World War, Germany was the most prosperous nation in Europe. It had the broadest industrial base, the most advanced technology, the most extensive transportation network, the most modern automobiles, the greatest number of universities, the best hospitals and TB sanatoriums, and so on. This high tide, moreover, was lifting all boats. Real wages and welfare benefits were everywhere rising. Accordingly, German socialism was thriving and settling in. In the 1911 parliamentary elections the SPD would become the largest political party in the land by gathering four and a half million votes and 110 seats in the Reichstag.

Meanwhile, however, a latent ideological dispute was simmering. It was touched off by Eduard Bernstein. During the period of the anti-socialist laws he had edited a journal, *Der Sozialdemokrat*, in his Zurich exile, whence it was smuggled into Germany. After 1890 he was free to circulate and in 1898 to publish his signature work, *Foundations of Socialism*, which trumpeted the doctrine of "revisionism." The message was simple: that the working class had more to gain from a sustained policy of reform within the existing political and economic structure than from a cataclysmic revolution intended to overthrow the capitalist state altogether. Sharply opposed to this revision of Marxist teachings were Karl Liebknecht (son of the old socialist warhorse Wilhelm Liebknecht) and the brilliant polemicist Rosa Luxemburg, who took a stand on the more radical wing of the party. Between these poles a compromise faction was formed by Karl Kautsky, who was soon joined by the veteran campaigner August Bebel. While these debates raged on during the prewar years, little was in fact accomplished to further either reform or revolution. One could point to stricter regulation of the working hours of women and children, wider insurance coverage for widows and orphans, or the somewhat increased compensation available through accident insurance. Yet the record of improvements was relatively sparse before 1914. Even a much heralded new insurance package for the entire Reich, enacted in 1911, fell lamentably short. As one scholar has astutely remarked, instead of uniting the three main existing forms of social security, this legislative measure in fact created a fourth. A glaring weakness also remained: the highly imperfect application of welfare programs in the countryside. No matter what criterion is applied—party activity, trade unionism, or social security benefits—German socialism remained a largely urban phenomenon, and it mostly affected the industrial labor force.

As noted, that force was nevertheless growing. It was for Germany the age of large factories. By one reckoning, in 1914 well over seven million persons were employed in firms with more than ten workers. As if by osmosis welfare was seeping into the population. Just before the war twenty-five million marks were being devoted annually to accident, illness, and disability insurance benefits for over half of German citizens. If there was a conspicuous flaw, it was the still flagging unemployment compensation, confined for the most part to some large municipalities and without a national framework. But that could be overlooked at a time of prosperity. Hence the international prestige of German social democracy was unshaken, even though the SPD was constantly isolated, frozen out by the reluctance of the imperial government to intervene more directly and forcefully in the legal or financial construction of what would later come to be called the welfare state.

These givens were significantly altered by the outbreak of war, which brought a sudden expansion of state power. The entire German nation was mobilized, meaning workers and peasants as well as soldiers. German socialists went along. For the first time in its history, by a margin of 78 to 14, the SPD voted for war credits. This action ignited a chain reaction that recalled the debate over revisionism in decades past. Those who supported national defense were appropriately called Majority Socialists (MSPD). Dissenters formed the Independent Social Democratic Party (USPD). And in 1916 an avowedly anti-war and anti-annexation group split off to found the Spartacus League, which soon became the Communist

Party of Germany (KPD). Obviously, to prosecute the war the government needed cooperation of the majority party and the trade unions, which was assured by a 1916 Reichstag resolution granting unions a role as the legitimate representatives of the labor movement.

Despite growing hardships, it is fair to observe that the national enthusiasm lasted until 1918. Wages declined. With more than half of men ages sixteen to fifty drafted into military service, the work force was necessarily augmented by elderly men, women, and children. Rationing meant poorer diets, sometimes hunger, and often nagging health problems. There was a notable rise in infectious diseases, especially tuberculosis. All of which put increasing strain on the existing welfare system. The result was a push for expanded benefits and more aid to struggling families—in a word, universalism, that is, health care for all citizens and not just certain social groups eligible within restrictive limits. Socialist party members and trade union officials actively supported this effort. Thus the war proved potentially favorable for an advance in social policy, not simply to meet special urgent needs for assistance but to establish the guarantee of a minimum standard for all. The welfare state was beginning to take shape.

For better and worse, no sequence of events served better to reveal the moderate and reformist character of German social democracy than the revolution of 1918. Once the war was irretrievably lost, the imperial regime simply collapsed. Kaiser Wilhelm II fled to Holland; the Bavarian monarch Ludwig III, to Austria. Other princes and their ministers scrambled while a fledgling republic was proclaimed. But what kind of republic? The immediate answer to that acute question rested largely with the socialists and with the so-called revolutionary councils (*Räte*) of soldiers, workers, and peasants that suddenly appeared throughout Germany. The six-month period after the Armistice of November 11 constitutes another intensively researched subject whose full complexity cannot be altogether unraveled here. But the most essential outcomes can be precisely defined. The vast majority of socialists stood with parliamentary democracy, and they even dominated the "revolutionary" councils. The moderate socialist leader Friedrich Ebert (who had lost two sons for his fatherland in the war) became the first president of the new Weimar Republic and promptly made a deal with General Wilhelm Groener to assure the restoration of law and order. With the assassination of Spartacist chiefs Karl Liebknecht and Rosa Luxemburg, the KPD was effectively eliminated from political leadership, while at a much ballyhooed Berlin conclave in December 1918 the councils effectively voted themselves out of existence, rejecting a Leninist soviet system by a decisive margin (400-52). In the parliamentary elections of January 1919 the majority SPD received a commanding 37.9 percent of the ballots cast. To sum up, with Social Democratic leadership Germany chose neither to return to a Kaiserreich nor to lurch forward to Bolshevism, opting instead for a centrist republic as the only viable future. Meanwhile, let it be added, the trade union movement flourished while its membership almost quadrupled from 1.2 million in 1917 to nearly 8 million by 1920.

A symptomatic sideshow was provided by simultaneous events in Bavaria. There the Wittelsbach dynasty was felled on 7 November 1918, two days before the Kaiser's flight from Berlin. The man who temporarily took charge, a Berlin Jewish journalist and Independent Socialist Kurt Eisner, was—to say the least—an anomaly in traditionally conservative and Catholic Bavaria. If in some sense of the term a revolutionary, Eisner was more of a Kantian than a Marxist, believing as he did in the ethical authority of socialism to bring a better world, or at least a more democratic Bavaria. Fittingly, he proposed a grand compromise: as before, Munich would host a bicameral legislature, but the previous Upper House of Lords would be replaced by representatives from the councils, while the Lower House (*Landtag*) remained composed of delegates elected from the existing political parties. When elections were held in January 1919, however, Eisner's USPD received less than 2 percent of the popular vote. Facing reality, he determined to resign, only to be assassinated on his way to the Landtag before he could do so. Chaos ensued. The Bavarian KPD under Eugen Leviné, a Jewish immigrant from Russia, took over and flew red flags from the twin towers of the Frauenkirche in downtown Munich. This revolt was rapidly quashed by an invading army and Free Corps militia troops in April 1919, bringing the German revolution to a bloody and definitive end.

It is of course relevant to note here that one individual present in Bavaria at the time of these tumultuous happenings was Adolf Hitler. Suffering the effects of poison gas on the Western Front, he was receiving medical treatment at a Bavarian army center in Rosenheim, just east of Munich. There he experienced a brief defiant encounter with a few members of the Red Guard, an incident reported in *Mein Kampf.* Subsequently he began his political career by speaking as an "enlightenment officer" at gatherings in Munich beerhalls. It was from this murky, overheated, smoke-filled atmosphere that National

Socialism was soon to emerge. From the beginning of Nazism, anti-communism and anti-Semitism were Hitler's oratorical specialties, for which figures like Eisner and Leviné offered perfect foils. Thus, needless to insist, his secular sermons owed little or nothing to mainstream social democracy but feasted instead on his fanatical opposition to socialism's more radical fringes.

As the Weimar Republic began, a renewed burst of enthusiasm for social reform was evident. It seemed that socialism's day had finally arrived. One obvious impetus was supplied by the return of needy war veterans, especially the wounded. There was initially much talk of "socialization," though no one knew precisely what that term implied. The SPD was at last freed from the political ghetto it had occupied during the Kaiserreich. But all of this did not last long, we know, and the Weimar Republic proved to be unstable and insecure, wracked as it was by runaway inflation in 1923 and then the disastrous effects of the Great Depression starting in 1929.

Two observations are in order. First, one must be struck by the continuity of German welfare legislation. The structure inherited from Bismarck's time was essentially left intact, and as before the socialists' efforts to promote unity and universality of welfare programs were unrequited. After all, there was little innovation. Second, some basic gains were nonetheless achieved. The eight-hour day was ratified in December 1923 in the wake of a currency reform that recast the German mark. In addition, a new compulsory unemployment insurance plan was introduced in 1927. That, however, turned out to be ineffective once the bottom fell out of the European economy two years later. Unemployment, which had hovered just over one million in mid-1929, reached more than six million by the onset of 1930. Until then wages had risen by a third since 1925, but now the bubble burst and the SPD reaped blame rather than credit. The staggering unemployment far exceeded the capacity of the state to cover insurance claims, so that the notion of social security became a bad joke. Hence it is unsurprising that the Weimar Republic's final years went badly for the socialist cause. The desperate Brüning and Papen governments were clearly anti-socialist and indeed arguably anti-parliamentarian altogether. The SPD's opposition to them was ineffectual, and the party's previous gains were all but nullified even before Adolf Hitler came to power. Social Democracy's moderation in the pursuit of public welfare ceased to be laudable and could instead be seen as a sign of weakness in coping with the nation's economic plight and the fierce attacks of rightist extremism.

Fascist Germany never developed a coherent social or economic policy after 1933. The Weimar system of social welfare was therefore not basically reorganized. But it was firmly controlled and administered by the Nazi state. This task was ostensibly relegated to the Deutsche Arbeitsfront (DAF) headed by Robert Ley. With the SPD outlawed and the socialist trade union movement disbanded, it was Ley's goal to unify everything under state authority as part of the process known as *Gleichschaltung*, a euphemism for nazification. In practice this was meant to ensure a militarization of the labor force in which workers were regarded as foot soldiers of the Third Reich. Everyone was to march to the same drum, regardless of class, as members of the national community. Not social reform but military rearmament was the Nazi priority, and Ley's program was largely ignored after the inception of Hermann Göring's Four-

Year Plan in 1936, which henceforth regulated production, wages, and working conditions, including price controls in 1939. Far from being an instrument of capitalism, as Karl Marx had posited, the state dictated the terms of society and economy. The one bright spot of this period was *Kindergeld*, that is, government assistance for mothers and their infants. Yet even that measure had its origin in racial and military policies of the Nazi party rather than a strong motive of social reform. Inevitably, the mobilization of an entire society for war raised the percentage of those covered by insurance, but those gains had nothing to do with the traditions of German socialism. And at war's end it all lay in a heap of rubble.

Insofar as healthcare and welfare were concerned, Germany did experience a "zero hour" (*Stunde Null*), as was evident at the unsuccessful Potsdam conference of Allied leaders in the late summer of 1945. Germany was splitting apart. Revived but sorely weakened, the socialist movement's immediate concern was to secure some insurance compensation for workers rather than to seek a fundamental reform. Beyond that, programmatically, the SPD hoped to rally its constituents to support a simplified and unified comprehensive system of social security—in a word *Einheitsversicherung*. There were two conspicuous obstacles. One was the question of how to pay for it after the trade unions balked at the notion that any newly enacted social legislation should be financed by higher contributions from workers rather than by progressive taxation. The other hurdle was the political disunity formalized by dividing the nation into four zones of occupation, one of which became the Soviet-dominated German Democratic Republic (known in the street by its German initials as the DDR). That entity, which was to exist for the next four decades, has been passed off rather too dismissively by one eminent historian as a mere footnote, but the DDR clearly served throughout the postwar era as a prod to the three soon united western zones, the *Bundesrepublik*, to promote more social welfare. It was the objective of the East German regime to promote socialism through a centralized state, meaning the unity and universality of social policy, yet without a complete break from German tradition. Most arresting were provisions of a 1968 reform for free medical care and hospital treatment without a term limit. An emphasis was also placed on old-age pensions and maternity care. The latter, which could not fail to recall Nazi propaganda of years past, was especially generous, allowing a pregnant female worker vacation with full pay for six weeks before and twenty weeks after giving birth. In that respect the DDR's only serious rival in the West was Sweden.

In the Bonn Republic, largely due to an SPD initiative, the 1891 law on old-age pensions was revised in 1957. This reform was isolated, however, and it basically retained the outlines of legislation under the Weimar Republic—or, more archly put, it was back to Bismarck. Rather than achieving a unification of insurance modes, therefore, the Bundesrepublik presided over the slow expansion of their various parts, which was eventually not inconsiderable: by the 1970s, it is estimated for example, provisions for illness insurance covered nearly 90 percent of the German population. Hence it was that, without a radical change of established structures, West Germany under socialist chancellors Willy Brandt and Helmut Schmidt encouraged the formation of a modern welfare state. This outcome was based on a fundamental compromise of establishing a broad social security network while leaving the existing capitalist system in place. Once more, as so often in the past, German social democracy thereby opted for a sensible centrist policy to which its adherents progressively rallied. After the fall of the Berlin wall in 1989 and the national reunification of Germany, the continuity of this resolution seemed assured. And, for its part, the SPD became a staple element of the secure parliamentary system, either as a loyal opposition or as part of a governing political coalition. By increments, without sparking a social upheaval, a German version of the welfare state had arrived.

# Chapter Three

## FRANCE

France's path to a welfare state was different from that of Germany in several fundamental regards. It may be useful to begin with a few generalizations about those differences, of which four stand out.

First of all, the French process of industrialization was much slower to develop. Accordingly, the progress of social reform and of socialism as a political movement came later than in Germany. It was not just that France had no Bismarck. Rather, before the end of the nineteenth century, the French economy simply lacked the preconditions of concentration and dynamism necessary to promote an imposing round of reformist activity that might have transformed the nation's welfare policies.

Second, the advance of socialism was more contentious in France. For one thing, the liberal doctrine of self-help, although never embodied in a single political party—or perhaps because of that—proved to be more pervasive and tenacious. At every hand liberals were therefore free to thwart the allegedly dangerous creed of socialism, and they were abetted in this resistance by the still considerable clout of the Catholic Church and by the stout opposition of countless independent entrepreneurs, to whom the French referred collectively as the *patronat*. As numerous historians have observed, France remained throughout the nineteenth century a land of individual property owners and small enterprises. For the French, it seems, small was decidedly beautiful, and to this day the word *petit* is a term of endearment in the French language. Notions of collectivism consequently did not fare well.

Third, the socialist camp itself suffered from a pronounced lack of unity. As in Germany, the spectrum of socialism was spread from moderate revisionists to doctrinaire revolutionaries. But there was a basic and obvious split between socialist political organizations and the trade union movement. While the former came to terms with the state in a republican consensus after 1870, the latter espoused radical syndicalism, encouraged social disruptions, and repeatedly threatened a general strike. French socialism was thus hobbled by a quarrelsome factionalism that endured to the First World War and beyond.

Moreover, finally, the French national circumstance was importantly influenced by its intimidating German neighbor, which served in social policy both as a model and as a polar opposite. French reformers well recognized the advantages of German social security measures, but these nonetheless appeared to them as unduly regimented and therefore unsuitable for the freedom-loving French. So they said. The principal hindrance was the doctrine of obligation, from which the French shrank back despite Germany's successful implementation of it. One other significant aspect of German influence can be quickly added here: the impact of the demographic imbalance that developed before 1914. While the German population surged to more than 65 million, the French count remained frozen below 40 million. This primary statistical fact helps to explain the inception of pronatalism in France and the emphasis placed there on assistance for maternity care, the lone beacon of prewar French social reform.

As for the party history of French socialism, there was little to report before the mid-nineteenth century. As always, France had more than its share of idealists, utopians, pseudo-socialists, and speculative intellectuals. Three names are invariably mentioned in that regard: Comte Henri de Saint-Simon, Charles Fourier, and Étienne Cabet—all contemporaries of Karl Marx. One other individual fits less comfortably into that list: Pierre-Joseph Proudhon, who wrote more pointed suggestions to deal with social problems and coined the biting dictum that "property is theft." He is the only one who drew a withering polemic from Marx, who made a caricature of Proudhon and then attacked the caricature. Marx knew a potential rival when he saw one. Another incipient socialist, Louis Blanc, enjoyed a brief but fruitless moment of celebrity with his "social workshops" during the insurrectionary events of 1848 in Paris. Otherwise there was no leftist political organization worthy of the name.

In the meantime, as was suitable for a nation whose population remained less than 50 percent urban (even by the most minimal definition of that term) and scattered mostly in small towns throughout 36,000 communes, social legislation was no more significant. So-called "welfare offices" (*bureaux de bienfaisance*) had been founded as far back as 1796 to offer assistance to the indigent. But they hardly functioned outside of a handful of cities and were everywhere regarded with suspicion by local notables as an invasion of Paris into the control of provincial affairs, as well as a threat to Catholic charities. The result was that orders from the capital about public health were often ignored and that representatives of the central state were avoided, just as provincials eluded tax collectors and military recruiters.

A different form of public assistance was promised by another welfare institution starting up before 1850. Mutual aid societies (*sociétés de secours mutuels*) were clusters of the working population that offered a kind of insurance against accidents, illness, and incapacity. Because voluntary, they coincided well enough with the liberal conception of self-help and "prudence" (*prévoyance*) based on individual responsibility. Yet they were usually local, small, expensive, and hence available only to a labor elite that could afford to pay the regular premiums. Besides, they declined to engage anyone with a pre-existing condition, notably tuberculosis, lest he break the bank (few females were admitted). These caveats notwithstanding, mutualism was to remain an important factor in French health care during the nineteenth century and into the twentieth.

The story of early social legislation was not brilliant and merits only a brief mention. In 1841 a provision was passed that forbad child labor under the age of eight (raised in 1874 to thirteen). In 1850 a national pension fund was created, but it was a flop, underfinanced and ineffective. The first accident insurance plan was not adopted before 1868, and it too languished until much later. In sum, the history of socialism and social welfare in France before 1870, as many writers have emphasized, seems to be one of retardation when compared with the western European norm. Moreover, one must account for the lost conflict against Bismarck's Prussia, the excesses of the Paris Commune, and the harsh state-directed repression of the French left by the early Third Republic. In retrospect, then, the Commune of 1871 does not appear to have been, as Karl Marx predicted, "the glorious harbinger of a new society," but rather the last episode of a popular sans-culottes insurrectionary tradition dating back to the French Revolution and including the June Days of 1848. Furthermore, if anything, it seems to have been more Proudhonian than Marxist in inspiration. French socialism consequently took some time to recover, and it did so haltingly.

The outlines of French socialism's rise as a political force in the decades before 1914 are clear and uncomplicated. The first congress of a socialist workers' party in France met in 1879. It was dominated by Jules Guesde, a self-professed Marxist ideologue. This gathering had little effect in the 1880s, but by 1893 socialist delegates of various stripes in the French parliament numbered forty. Their disunity continued through the tempest of the Dreyfus Affair, from which they emerged largely in support of a republican consensus under the leadership of the Radical (that is, liberal) Party. The principal challenge to this general orientation came from Germany, land of the largest and most prestigious labor movement in Europe. The issue was ministerialism: specifically, whether a socialist deputy, Alexandre Millerand, could serve as minister in a liberal bourgeois cabinet. That question was decided negatively in 1904 under heavy German pressure at an international socialist conference in Amsterdam, where the more intransigent Guesdist position triumphed. That decision was short-lived. The year 1905 saw the formation of a new unified socialist political movement, the Section Française de l'Internationale Ouvrière (SFIO), under the moderate and astute tutelage of Jean Jaurès. It was Jaurès's task during most of the ensuing decade to maintain a centrist position despite the beckoning of radical syndicalism within the French trade unions. An eloquent orator, educated at the École Normale Supérieure, a convinced republican, Jaurès succeeded in eclipsing Guesde and in promoting a Gallic type of socialist revisionism. There was another factor. Jaurès was a pacificist, a stance that proved increasingly troublesome as the clouds of war gathered and that undoubtedly provoked his assassination in 1914 at a Paris café. Thereupon the SFIO was swept uncertainly into the wartime political truce known as the *union sacrée*. As elsewhere, nationalism trumped socialism in the war years.

It was symptomatic of the prewar period that mutualism flourished as never before. By 1900 there were over 13,000 mutual aid societies with a membership of nearly two million, loosely grouped under the Mutualist Charter of 1898. This rapid growth had implications. It meant that the liberal doctrine of self-help and individual responsibility could resist anything that smacked of socialism. It meant that the French *patronat* held the upper hand over labor and that only an urban working-class elite could expect to receive a substantial social assistance. Yet it also meant that mutual aid societies became more and more dependent on state subsidies to meet the ever growing costs of health care and social welfare measures.

Such measures were infrequent but not inconsequential during the prewar years. One reason for legislative lethargy was the appearance of a new actor on the political stage: solidarism. This movement (not actually a party), led by Léon Bourgeois, which sought a middle way between capitalist liberalism and nascent socialism, was an attempt to blunt the political thrust of both. In 1886 Henri Monod, a collaborator of Bourgeois, became the director of public assistance in the Ministry of the Interior, and two years later he had a hand in creating the Conseil Supérieur de l'Assistance Publique, which sponsored reform legislation in the 1890s. The results were mediocre. In 1892 a bill was adopted that favored maternity assistance and child care. This was driven, as noted, mostly by a fear of depopulation vis-à-vis Germany, an apprehension of decadence firmly based on disturbing facts: between the censes of 1891 and 1911 France added an annual average of 63,000 citizens; Germany, 500,000. In 1893 a national program of Assistance Médicale Gratuite was inaugurated, but barely a third of French communes had affiliates, and many of them existed only on paper. A plan for old-age poverty assistance arrived in 1905, yet this measure had the effect of extending traditional charity rather than replacing it. Finally, in 1910 an obligatory pension plan was approved by the French parliament, theoretically a bold step toward a national welfare system. Yet the most authoritative historian of this topic has described the new law as a "dead letter," and the Caisse Nationale des Retraites remained a shadow before 1914. Furthermore, socialist efforts to establish a minimum wage repeatedly failed. Nor did Jean Jaurès have any better luck with his call for the universalist principle of "a pension for all."

Looking back, it is not difficult to assemble a laundry list of obstacles on which reformist intentions foundered. Chief among them was the toxic notion of obligation, seemingly antithetical to the French way of life and stoutly opposed by mutual aid societies, local notables, organized groups of the *patronat*, and the Catholic Church. In addition, there was the intractable conundrum of finance, whether by direct and indirect taxation or by some contributory arrangement. There were also problems of eligibility, implementation, and administration of welfare offices throughout France, especially in rural areas.

The participation of French socialism in all of the above may be simply summarized. The majority of the SFIO consistently opted to join in the republican consensus to advance democracy and public welfare measures in the conviction that selective and capricious charity or mutual aid should be replaced by the right of every citizen to an assured minimum existence. The gains realized by this effort, it bears repeating, were mostly on paper—all the more so as the war approached and nationalism prevailed, symbolized by the election of Raymond Poincaré to the republican presidency in 1913. On balance, then, the rhetoric of class struggle, frequent strikes notwithstanding, considerably exceeded actual performance. The more mundane reality was bargaining, voting, and scratching out modest concessions, none of which came close to the German-style obligation of an individual mandate with extensive state regulation.

In more than one respect, the First World War proved to be a pivotal moment. We saw that, as the conflict began, the myth of a general strike, long fomented by the socialist trade unions, was swamped by wartime nationalism and the *union sacrée*. Even Jules Guesde sat in the French cabinet. Suspicion of state intervention gave way to public assistance and health insurance, the need for which was all too obvious in a struggle that killed 1.4 million Frenchmen and left another 3 million injured, many of them permanently disabled. The return of war veterans from the front gave new impetus to care for the unemployed and others in distress. At last, across the countryside, *la patrie* began to mean something. France felt an obligation to catch up in welfare and population growth. Hence nationalism and natalism became closely associated, and the French were to be leaders in European family social planning after 1918. In short, the war showed that voluntary efforts of the past were inadequate and that state intervention was essential. The war had brought new taxes, and they would be retained afterwards. Indicatively, mutual aid societies lost nearly a million members, and even a postwar numerical correction could not mask mutualism's gradual marginalization. Instead, state bureaucracy expanded, which before had been painfully lacking for health care, and new hospitals sprouted everywhere, first for wounded veterans, then for other citizens. Still imperfectly realized, the beginnings of a welfare state were thus unmistakably stirred by the First World War.

Yet the interwar years brought more disappointment. French public assistance programs became neither universal nor uniform. First, the French could not surmount the hump of obligation, meaning a state-imposed individual mandate compelling all citizens to join a national health and welfare scheme. This proposal could easily be attacked as either too Germanic or too Bolshevist. But the basic problem was the lack of a broad and firm republican consensus.

As it turned out, solidarism was not so solid, and socialism spoke with a cacophony of discordant voices. Second, French reformers failed to unify the existing institutions of public welfare into a single system. Social reform therefore remained a ramshackle edifice, bits and pieces, so that improvement of this or that aspect of legislation was without general effect.

That said, it is hyperbolic to speak of these as the "hollow years" or to portray France as a "stalemate society," as prominent scholars have done. The record of reform was not that bleak. Especially in some of the larger cities social reformers were able to create mini-welfare states. Necessarily such changes were piecemeal, but they showed that the First World War had been a catalyst and that in welfare France was beginning to catch up. In 1921 the French parliament began to consider a German-type of compulsory social security. One spur to do so was the return of Alsace-Lorraine by the Treaty of Versailles. Citizens of that area had benefited from German social legislation since 1871, and they were unwilling to forego it after 1918. The French nation would need to integrate and adapt to the returned territories. This effort, however, was stymied by an informal alliance of employers, mutual aid societies, and medical doctors (who were fearful of state interference with fee-for-service billing and the control of hospitals). Nearly a decade elapsed before a bill was adopted between 1928 and 1930 to increase illness insurance, maternity care, disability benefits, and modest pensions. Mutual aid societies were integrated into this reform, in which they essentially served as insurance agencies, further magnifying their dependency on state subsidies. The effect was salutary albeit still woefully incomplete: between 1930 and 1940 coverage of the French citizenry rose from 30 percent to over 50 percent. That trend could be measured by other statistics. The portion of public assistance in the national budget, which stood at only 7 percent in 1930 (half that of Germany) rose to well over 11 percent by the mid-1940s.

Not coincidentally, this growth occurred during a time when larger industrial enterprises were becoming more common. In 1906 nearly 60 percent of French workers were engaged in firms with less than ten employees; two decades later that figure had dropped to 40 percent. Ironically, some of the opposition to reformist social policy came from laborers in small traditional enterprises, those who stood to profit most. Yet it cannot be said that between the wars France experienced a thrilling take-off to a new stage of capitalism. Rather, the nation continued a steady evolution toward advanced industrialization, all of which helps to explain the persistence of French liberalism and the confounding impediments to socialism.

In political life this circumstance corresponded to two notable developments. Liberalism had been increasingly embodied by the Radical Party since its founding in 1901. This new grouping proved to be both successful and crucial. By the early 1930s the Radicals claimed 166 delegates in the Chamber of Deputies and nearly a third of senators. Importantly, the party quietly shed its former emphasis on self-help and accepted the necessity of government regulation and financial intervention. It was therefore able to find more affinity with the socialists, as was evidenced by agreeing to such measures as better social insurance, paid vacations for workers, and a further reduction of working hours. In the meantime socialism was undergoing a more raucous transformation. At the congress of Tours in 1920 both the party and the trade unions split apart. Almost 70 percent of members present voted to follow the French Communist Party (PCF) in joining the Third International, and French trade unions found themselves simultaneously confronted with new and more radical pro-communist counterparts. But this show of leftist strength turned out to be something of an optical illusion. Under the skillful leadership of Léon Blum the SFIO regained its bearings and plurality, and in the mid-1930s the party joined with the Radicals and (with reservations) Communists in a Popular Front. After assuming the premiership, Blum signed the Matignon accords that created a forty-hour working week, granted a 12 to 15 percent salary increase to workers, and assured state protection for union activity and collective bargaining. French socialism had reached a high-water mark, and the future seemed bright.

We know that the sequel was otherwise. All of this apparent progress was attained in the shadow of a menacing Nazi Germany. Blum was seen by many of his countrymen as a latter-day Jean Jaurès, but there was one crucial difference: he was not a pacifist. He expended much of his energy to shore up the French economy and military to be competitive. The French franc was devalued in 1936, yet unemployment rose while prices and deficits climbed. By 1938 Blum was prime minister no more, as the Popular Front collapsed and Radical leaders like Paul Reynaud and Édouard Daladier took charge. The results were soon to appear in the form of the Munich agreements and the ensuing disastrous military defeat in the summer of 1940. Four years of German occupation followed.

It goes without insisting that the political scene in Vichy France was hardly normal. Socialist and communist leaders were exiled, isolated, or arrested, while their parties were eliminated.

Trade unions were outlawed and disbanded. There were no political campaigns or elections. Attempts were meanwhile made to integrate France into the new European economic order directed from Berlin. This would matter in the long run because so many French employers collaborated with the Occupation authorities and would later be discredited, therefore unable to mount opposition of postwar welfare measures. Progress in that direction remained theoretical but not insignificant. Like its predecessors, the Pétain regime emphasized family allowances and thereby sought to foster a national compensation plan, which, though unsuccessful at the time, helped to set an agenda for postwar France. Likewise, in 1941 the Vichy government declared public hospitals open to all citizens. Again, despite having limited immediate effect, this policy set a theoretical precedent that was to be ratified in 1945. Most interesting was the story of social insurance, for which planning was launched by Pierre Laroque at Vichy. Ousted from government service on racial grounds, he fled to London to aid the Gaullist cause there and joined with a group that set out to devise a unified social security scheme on the basis of compulsory participation by all French wage-earners. It was this universalist conception that Laroque and others brought back to liberated Paris in August 1944 as a blueprint for the Fourth Republic

From the preceding survey of French socialism and social legislation since the mid-nineteenth century it is evident that the welfare state underwent a prolonged period of gestation. But there was no smooth path forward. The war years had created a complete rupture, with both the Third Republic (for its inglorious collapse) and the Vichy regime (for its fawning collaboration) thoroughly disgraced. If ever there was a moment to start anew, this was it. The exiled Laroque team in London returned to France with plans to found a veritable *sécurité sociale*, that is, a health care and welfare program for all based on an obligatory individual mandate. Thus on 22 May 1946 the Caisse Nationale de Sécurité Sociale was created. Alas, it did not quite work out as Laroque hoped. The medical profession was one problem: patients demanded to choose their own physician and physicians required the freedom to set fees, arrangements at odds with a unified system and controlled costs. Mutual aid societies, compromised by their collaboration with the Vichy regime and long accustomed to an ethic of voluntarism, were also reluctant to cooperate. And the administration of the CNSS was left to regional insurance boards, often dominated by the CGT trade unionists. Such complexities meant that the French did not adopt a truly universal structure in which all citizens were included on equal terms (like the British National Health Service). Instead, they added another layer of welfare institutions on top of prewar legislation. The immediate effect was to increase coverage of the citizenry from 50 percent to about 70 percent by 1960. That was to integrate the majority of the French population into a social welfare system that still left some room for private insurance companies and for the agency of mutual aid societies, an outcome that fell short of the expectations of both Laroque's crew and leaders of the SFIO.

The rest of the Fourth Republic was a pause while loopholes were gradually closed. In 1947 a compulsory plan extended coverage for workers in commerce, manufacturing, and the liberal professions—although many were reluctant to comply with the requirement of a contribution via payroll taxation. In the year following an autonomous plan was adopted for agricultural workers, artisans, and some industrial laborers. The patchwork character of these measures was further illustrated by a separate allowance for large families. The notion of "coverage" varied considerably, more or less depending on an individual's ability to afford a supplementary insurance policy. But generally included was compensation for hospital stays, dentistry, prescription drugs, and disability costs. One striking lacuna in France was still the absence of a comprehensive unemployment insurance plan, which did not become law until 1958.

By that time the Fourth Republic had run its course, and Charles de Gaulle reentered the political scene with a seven-year presidential mandate as the head of the Fifth Republic. The leftist parties were severely weakened. The socialists were reduced from 97 to 44 delegates in the Chamber of Deputies, and the communists from 149 to 10. The conservative governments of De Gaulle, Georges Pompidou, and Valérie Giscard d'Estaing were thus free to manage and embellish the various programs that had already been established in the first postwar decade. By the 1980s an estimated 96 percent of the French populace was covered by one plan or another, despite the pockets of resistance to mandatory social security and the objections from physicians to undue state interference. Throughout, one basic problem recurred: the difficulty of imposing a contributory social policy, that is, a compulsory financing of reform measures through earnings-related premiums rather than (as in Britain and Sweden) progressive taxation. This had the paradoxical effect of inciting some workers and other wage-earners to oppose a universalist social security system. Hence, in all, the French case was marked by slow and irregular progress rather than a dramatic burst of reform legislation. Rather, the French resolution of the social question was a mixture of taxation and contributory regulations and a gradual reorganization of insurance procedures by regions. With time, the record shows, socialists and other political factions came to accept this elaborate arrangement.

Social policy gains in France were thus incremental and inconsistent rather than sudden and definitive. The same was true under the socialist president François Mitterand as well as the more conservative government of Jacques Chirac. By the final decade of the twentieth century 99 percent of the French people had some form of coverage and paid for their social security benefits mostly through a payroll tax (rather than income tax as in Scandinavia). It was under the socialist premier Lionel Jospin that an all-embracing Couverture Médicale Universelle (CMU) was enacted to bring in the last of stragglers. As so often, the CMU was tucked onto the existing *sécurité sociale* rather than effecting a huge structural change. And again the curiosity was that lingering opposition was often due to the distaste of trade unions for the principle of universality, which they saw as a challenge to their heretofore privileged status in welfare legislation.

The impending crisis of the early twenty-first century, not in France alone, was that welfare costs were rising as coverage was extended to an aging population, a squeeze that tended to raise expenses and contract receipts. Evidently the welfare state, the *État-Providence*, has its limits. The question of adequately underwriting French social security remains open. In any event, the achievement of social democracy in France can now been seen as a successful compromise among the republican state, industrial employers, and the organized labor force. Certainly this social contract has not produced an egalitarian society. There are still rich and poor, wealthy capitalists and wage-earning workers. But inequality has been reduced and an enduring social harmony realized.

# Chapter Four

# BRITAIN

In its splendid isolation, Great Britain was unlike continental Europe. First, of course, it had—at least since 1066 and all that—an invulnerable military protection both because of the waters that surrounded the British Isles and the superiority of its powerful naval fleet. Second, until the mid-nineteenth century, Britain possessed an unrivaled worldwide empire, which meant among other things that it constituted a unique one-nation trading block in Europe that was less dependent than other nations on commerce with proximate neighbors. And third, of particular relevance here, the English experienced an early burst of industrialization in the late eighteenth century, especially in textiles and metals, which produced the exhilaration of an unparalleled boom of wealth and of population growth, thereby creating before 1850 a higher standard of living than could be found on the Continent.

Yet the curiosity was that these unmatched advantages did not induce a pioneering effort of welfare legislation. Before the 1830s the English record of social reform was virtually blank—except for the infamous Poor Laws, dating from 1601, which inadequately dealt with the chronic problems of poverty and unemployment. They were administered on a local scale through towns, parishes, and counties with a notable lack of state intervention or subvention, some exception made for London. Beyond that, the rule was friendly societies (counterparts to the French mutual aid societies) and a smattering of voluntary private insurance programs.

The period between 1830 and 1850 witnessed a flurry of rather meager reform measures. In 1833 a Factory Act was passed that restricted child labor under the age of eight. In the year following the Poor Law Amendment Act encouraged the merger of poverty relief agencies into the Poor Law Union, a feeble attempt to overcome localism. Successive enactments in the late 1840s further limited hours of labor by imposing a twelve-hour standard for male workers and a maximum of ten for women and children. Enforcement of these regulations, initially confined for the most part to textiles and mining, was extended in 1867 to other branches of industrial production, which meant enlarging the state's team of inspectors and promoting more bureaucratic centralization in the form of a Poor Law Board. Evidently, then, Britain remained largely a land of laissez-faire until near century's end, with nothing comparable to the comprehensive social legislation of Bismarckian Germany.

One modest reform breakthrough came in the 1880s and 1890s as labor groups began to form and apply pressure in favor of no-fault insurance, especially in mining and railroad construction. This move culminated in the 1897 Workmen's Compensation Act that folded all industrial labor accidents into a no-fault system. Meanwhile, a former coal miner, Keir Hardie, founded the Independent Labour Party—but, lacking mass appeal, it soon flamed out. At the same time, a brilliant cluster of socialist intellectuals coalesced as the Fabian Society. That name said everything. This clique (not a political party), which boasted such illustrious members as Sidney and Beatrice Webb as well as George Bernard Shaw and George Orwell, was named after a Roman general, Quintus Fabius, renowned for his cautious tactics. Finally, as the new century began, the modern Labour Party was established with the express purpose of promoting workers' rights and benefits through the legislative process, hardly a program of revolutionary intent. Predictably, as a political movement Labour came to display a close alignment of party and trade unions, a tendency to consort with reformist liberals against the conservatives, and only a faint connection between progressive social theorists and industrial workers.

It was indicative that the first decade of the twentieth century saw a surge of friendly societies. They had far more than twice as many members (about five and a half million) as the trade unions. More British workers voted with the liberals than with the Labour Party. Hence progress in social reform was hesitant and, it seemed, half-hearted. Yet, after all, something was percolating. In 1905 an Unemployment Workmen Act represented the first state attempt to counter that industrial scourge, and 1908 saw the British Old Age Pension Act, which offered social aid to citizens over seventy years, in effect repudiated the Poor Laws, and advanced the first halting step to a welfare state. This legislation was notable for two features that were eventually to characterize English social reform, distinct from Germany: from the outset it was conceived as a universalist measure for all, and it was financed through general taxation. In the main it was the accomplishment of so-called "new liberalism," starring David Lloyd George and Winston Churchill, abetted to be sure by the Labour Party. One caveat is due. Although he made a much publicized trip to Germany in 1908 to study implementation of Bismarck's social legislation, Lloyd George did not return to advocate its contributory means of finance. But, impressed by what he saw, he did push disability insurance, particularly for victims of tuberculosis. Thus in Britain (as in Germany, not in France) a serious TB sanatorium and dispensary movement was set in motion before the First World War.

All of which brought a sea change to British social policy in 1911. The National Insurance Act (NIA) of that year created an obligatory sickness and unemployment insurance plan "from cradle to grave" and earned for Lloyd George the perhaps unsought sobriquet of his nation's Bismarck. Actually this enactment promised to create even more control of public welfare by national state agencies than existed in Germany. It meant more uniform regulations, more state inspectors, and broader coverage, including small workshops, for instance, and domestic help. The persistent problem, however, was tepid financing through flat-rate premiums, which mandated a complex system of tripartite contributions from employers, workers, and the state. For the time being, friendly societies and private insurance plans were left intact, the immediate result of which was a mixture of compulsory and voluntary arrangements. In sum, Britain was gradually laying the foundation of a coherent social policy, although it lagged fully thirty years behind Germany in doing so.

Postwar British social welfare reform bore little resemblance to the prewar. As elsewhere in Europe, carnage of the war provided a strong stimulus to state-sponsored assistance for the injured and indigent. And in 1921 fiscal shortfalls caused the British to drop flat-rate contributory financing that had been the basis of the 1911 NIA, a basic change in the structure of public welfare procedures. In 1925 this measure was joined by a pension plan for widows and orphans, therewith closing a conspicuous legislative loophole. By the 1930s Britain had thus tentatively entered onto a path toward a national health system that would not depend on private insurance programs to fill in the gaps.

These developments, realized mainly under liberal aegis, owed relatively little to support offered by the Labour Party. Not until 1922 was Ramsay McDonald elected the party's leader, which he had unofficially been since 1906. Then in 1924 he became the first Labour prime minister and foreign secretary, but his was a minority government dependent on the support of liberals. He proved to be a successful champion of public education, but he had no solution for high unemployment (over a million), and his cabinet promptly fell in 1925. McDonald had another brief residency at 10 Downing Street at the end of the 1920s, until he was forced out again in 1931, this time by his own party. From that point on, up to the Second World War, Britain muddled through with a series of coalitions in which conservatives, liberals, and labourites were fairly evenly matched. Although the Great Depression boosted unemployment further to two and a half million, those who had jobs fared not badly, since prices fell and real wages consequently increased. British exports remained strong, and the social agitation of trade unions posed no threat to national unity.

After 1939 the last vestiges of laissez-faire were abandoned in favor of what has appropriately been called "war socialism." Britain was literally under siege, a spur to state intervention and a spirit of cooperation among classes. Tax rates that had been elevated from 10 percent to over 30 percent during the First World War were retained, so that direct taxation accounted for nearly half of state revenues. Before 1945, as it turned out, the British government thus became the employer of almost half of the population.

Enter William Beveridge. At first a minor bureaucrat in London, he slipped through the crack between the Labour Party and the liberals. He gained support from the Fabian Society before 1914, yet he also became a member of Winston Churchill's staff at the Board of Trade and thereby entered the national scene. His central idea was simple: a scheme of universal social security such as that advocated by Sidney and Beatrice Webb. The First World War had not generated expectations sufficient for its realization then, but the Second did. As that conflict ended, Churchill was surprisingly ousted from the prime ministry by the socialist candidate Clement Attlee (393 parliamentary seats to 210), and the stage was set for creation of the British National Health Service (NHS) in 1948. Thanks in large part to the efforts of Aneurin Bevan, a Welsh socialist who served as Attlee's Minister of Health, the Labour government from 1945 to 1951 laid the foundation of a welfare state that still exists, based on the Beveridge Plan of 1942.

With this unapologetic single-payer system Great Britain vaulted past France and Germany in the march to unified social security. It did not do so without criticism or opposition. In a long tradition of principled protest, not alone in Britain, the British Medical Association was especially hostile to what it portrayed as unwarranted state interference into private medical practice. And there has been no shortage of complaints about delays and inefficiencies in the system. Yet the novelty and security of costless hospital treatment and physician care have clearly outweighed those reservations. Moreover, the NHS was accompanied during the Attlee administration by a wave of nationalization in other key sectors of the British economy: radio, aviation, railways, electrical and coal industries, etc.

One cannot overlook one great difference and one striking similarity between Britain's welfare solution and that of Germany. The difference was a rupture with the past in the United Kingdom, unlike the German tendency to add layer upon layer to the Bismarckian foundation with sustained continuity. The inescapable similarity was controversy about modes of payment. Initially, the Beveridge reforms were hobbled by an inadequate contributory flat-rate system, which was thought retrogressive by elements of the Labour Party. This tension led to the resignation from the Attlee cabinet by the trade union leader Ernest Bevin, who had been the wartime Minister of Labour and who drummed together a left-wing movement in favor of direct progressive taxation. Thus the Labour Party and the trade unions were at odds for a time until the financial weakness of the Beveridge Plan became apparent along with a need to seek new financial resources. The result was an agonizing reappraisal by the party, a drift away from the flat-rate conception to a more Bismarckian type of earnings-related scheme, and a widespread acceptance of greater state participation and control. Yet Beveridge's basic principle of universalism—that is, coverage for all—remained the same. The superannuated notion of self-help was finally buried, even by the liberals, as Britain embraced a social compact that featured not only a reconciliation of political extremes—never remarkably extreme in Britain—but also the positive support of the broad middle class. Both were forthcoming within the traditional British context of a stable constitutional monarchy, parliamentary democracy, and a thriving but moderate labor movement. To generalize: whereas social policy in Germany was crafted largely to meet demands and implicit or explicit threats of radicalism within working-class organizations, in Great Britain welfare legislation evolved primarily as a consensual solution to the nagging social questions of poverty, incapacity, and inequality.

Finally, one ancillary issue deserves mention here. It is of course impossible to measure the actual influence of Britain's most famous economist of the twentieth century, John Maynard Keynes. Yet, at least in a general sense, he surely deserves some credit as the patron of a peaceful and more equitable society guaranteed by an active state. In this regard his vision for Great Britain and the West was directly contrary to that of Karl Marx, for whom society could only progress through a series of conflicts. For Keynes the stability and adaptability of capitalism were axiomatic, and hence the need for social compromises. Precisely that intellectual cornerstone accorded with the deepest aspirations and doctrines of British socialism.

# Chapter Five

## SWEDEN

Sweden was a latecomer to social welfare, and there are several obvious reasons why that was so. The Swedish nation occupied a vast remote Nordic space, which meant that it contained a relatively large and scattered rural population with little urban industry throughout the nineteenth century. Its major products were principally raw materials like iron ore and lumber, both of superior quality, apt for export. Agricultural interests were thus a challenge to liberal principles within the context of a retarded industrialization. A Social Democratic Party was not founded until 1889, and it long remained behind the curve, usually receiving and eventually adopting reforms rather than originating them.

The paradoxical circumstance of Swedish socialism, then, was that the party initially sought reforms for an industrial working class in a nation that was still largely rural. Gradually it came around to a more universalist platform that included agricultural labor. Because so many of those who worked in rural areas were self-employed farmers or loggers, they took a dim view of a contributory system in which organized urban laborers alone benefited from payments by their employers. The solution had to be taxation, and Swedish socialists slowly came to realize it.

Given this circumstance, the nineteenth century was a time of gridlock, since the weight of rural Sweden was sufficient to thwart social legislation like Bismarck's that would have concentrated benefits on the urban working class. Yet Germany did provide some stimulus for reform. In 1884 a move started for a Swedish social insurance scheme, but, as indicated, sharp disagreements immediately surfaced about the broadness of coverage and the means of financing it. Unable to resolve such disputes, reform efforts proved futile until a 1905 initiative, mainly by liberals, for state-financed uniform pensions without employer or employee contributions. An Old Age Pensions Commission was formed in 1907, which sifted through the inherent contradictions of reform proposals before rendering its belated report in 1912. The Commission's recommendations amounted to a rejection of German precedents in favor of a universalist approach deemed more suitable for Sweden. Financing remained the core issue, however, and some allowance had to be made for contributions of varying grades. This compromise became law in 1913 with a pension plan thus made available to all Swedish citizens, a universalist scheme potentially much more thoroughgoing and radical than anything imagined or implemented under Bismarck. With dubious justification, the Social Democratic Party of Sweden assumed full credit for this measure, which in truth represented a sensible arrangement between socialists and agrarians. Above all, it represented a basic shift away from liberalism and also a decisive revision of orthodox Marxism.

The parallel political history of Swedish socialism can best be evaluated in this light. The party leader from 1907 to his death in 1925 was Hjalmar Branting. From a young Marxist firebrand he evolved into the very image of moderation. He became the first Swedish socialist in parliament in 1896 and later the first socialist prime minister in 1920. As a champion of revisionism, he became Sweden's Eduard Bernstein, ultimately advocating universalism, a larger role of the state, and a heavier burden of direct and indirect taxation. Thereby he led Swedish socialists away from a contributory German model by emulating and even surpassing the British example. It bears repeating, nonetheless, that much of the pre-1914 reform impetus was inherited and not generated by the socialist leadership under Branting.

The socialist record between the world wars was inchoate. Branting was twice able to form a shaky Social Democratic minority government between 1920 and 1924, but to little effect. From 1924 to 1932 a liberal-conservative coalition governed. The Great Depression brought labor disputes and strikes, the return of a socialist-agrarian coalition, and frustrating efforts to curb raging unemployment. Two events in 1938 were noteworthy. One was a change in the tax code, allowing business firms to deposit half of their profits into the Swedish Central Bank in return for tax breaks. Suddenly the government had cash. Also in that year the so-called Saltsjöbaden Agreement was struck, a deal between employers and socialist trade unions that promised a calmer era of negotiations and government mediation. This truce prevailed through the ensuing war years, although it did not totally preclude conflicts between labor and management or industrial workers and public sector employees.

Reforms that had begun in 1913 and then irregularly augmented in the 1930s were able to sweep the boards after the Second World War as Sweden (along with Denmark) clearly emerged as the avatar of European social welfare, beginning with a basic pension bill in 1946. With its relatively sparse (about 7 million at that time) and ethnically homogeneous population, Sweden realized possibilities that other nations could only dream of: generous pensions, costless medical care, adequate compensations and family allowances. The fundamental principle of universalism was not unknown elsewhere, especially in Britain, but its implementation in Sweden exceeded the rest. In large measure this welfare progress was due to the remarkably long tenure of the Social Democratic Party. Its postwar chief, Tage Erlander, was prime minister from 1946 to 1969, that is, for twenty-three consecutive years! His protégé, Olaf Palme, then headed the party from 1969 until his shocking assassination in downtown Stockholm in 1986. Palme's electoral defeat in the late 1970s closed a span of four uninterrupted decades of socialist domination. And his party returned for an encore from 1982 to 2006. There had been no comparable continuity since Bismarck's decades as Prussian prime minister and German chancellor in the late nineteenth century.

As was to be expected, many Swedish socialists—including Tage Erlander himself—expressed reservations about a universalist policy that benefited the rich as well as the poor. But the majority of Swedes supported the emerging welfare system, and the socialists acceded—not before gaining a few significant concessions. Insurance premiums for the wealthy were doubled, and a draconian inheritance tax was introduced, presumably on the theory that lavish social benefits through the state made an accumulation of private family wealth unnecessary. Hence the welfare state in Sweden was not without its Robin Hood aspects.

In 1953 a compulsory health insurance law was codified. Obligatory for every citizen, this measure violated the principle of uniformity insofar as compensation for illness and incapacity were henceforth to be reckoned on an earnings-related scale, not by flat rates. This stipulation passed with the enthusiastic approval of trade unions, whereas rural interests—ineluctably weakened by the development of a more industrialized and urban society—lost their argument for a simple flat-rate scheme. To that extent, yet again, it was back to Bismarck. Indisputably, this victory of the unions somewhat contradicted the universalist model, but national solidarism has nevertheless been more fully attained by Sweden than Germany, France, or Britain.

It helps to be rich. And no other block of nations is as wealthy as Scandinavia. After the discovery of offshore oil fields, Norway has the highest per capita income in the world. Sweden, Denmark, and Finland are not far behind. However, these countries are also among the most highly taxed. The question is: what do they receive for their money? Which is at the same time to ask: what does a genuine welfare state look like? A closer look at the social benefits in Sweden should help to provide answers.

The basic principle of the Swedish welfare system is that all citizens have a right to adequate health care. The system is administered mostly through twenty county and 290 municipal councils. It is thus decentralized, but its agencies function under uniform national regulations and central state supervision. This arrangement is supplemented in some cases by individual fee-for-service medical care. Financed largely through a combination of direct taxation and indirect levies on consumption (for example, of alcoholic beverages), Swedish welfare is sweeping, solidarist, but also expensive. Basic health and medical care constitutes at least 10 percent of the gross domestic product, and by 1980 the total cost of all welfare measures in Sweden had reached nearly 30 percent of the national GDP.

This broad and elaborate structure truly realizes the oft quoted but seldom achieved slogan of cradle to grave. Childbirth and care of toddlers is well provided for. Maternity leave is generous. Parents have an allowance of 480 days of paid leave before a child reaches the age of eight, an option of course usually taken by mothers but also, up to 20 percent, by fathers. Additional child support is available for all sick or disabled children living in Sweden, including recent immigrants. A separate housing fund has been established for poor families with children. Public education from kindergarten through high school is free. Subsidized by the state, costs for vocational and university training are modest, with scholarships provided for the needy.

There is an extensive program of adult education, especially for the English language, a basic competence in which is mandatory for all Swedish students and adults. Illness and disability assistance are offered, the expense of which during an initial fortnight is paid by employers, thereafter by state insurance. Unemployment relief is likewise part of the welfare system. More significant and fundamental are pension funds for the elderly, who can choose to retire at age sixty-one. Their degree of compensation depends in part on length of employment and level of previous income, not a flat rate. Funded care for the elderly can be arranged either at home or in retirement centers. For all of these matters and more, further information is readily available on the Internet and in the abundant scholarly literature.

All in all, the results are impressive. Sweden is the leading nation of the world in income equality. It has one of the lowest rates of infant mortality: about one in 100,000. Swedish life expectancy is nearly eighty for men and over eight-three for women, virtually unmatched. Of the now nine and a half million Swedes, none is neglected or left uncovered, uneducated, or wanting for adequate health care. Admittedly, this laudable outcome has only been made possible by a century of social legislation that required difficult choices, financial sacrifices, and personal restrictions in a setting particularly favorable for a universalist approach to solving the inherent social problems of modernity. Still, there is no more admirable example of the welfare state.

# Chapter Six

## UNITED STATES

"Amerika, Du hast es besser," wrote Goethe. Naturally that assertion is debatable from a number of standpoints, none of them more egregious than public health care. The well known truth is that, to date, the United States has in the realm of welfare legislation developed nothing comparable to the more advanced states of Europe. Decidedly, then, the USA is the perpetual outlier in this story, for it seems that social inequality is deeply embedded in the American experience and the American character. Explanations of that observation are plentiful, of course, and attempts to untangle them are not wanting. Here they may be limited to four elementary factors.

First there is geography. Not only is the United States far separated by sea from Europe, it contains a space many times larger than any European nation, a territory extensive enough to match the entirety of that continent west of the Urals. America was populated, moreover, largely by people who had turned their backs on the Old

World. In the nineteenth century it was still a young nation, ever expanding westward across open vistas, where settlers appropriately embraced a miasmic frontier ethic of rugged individualism—not exactly fertile soil for socialistic reforms.

To this, secondly, one must add America's inherent ethnic diversity. That bedrock included not only all those various European immigrants who continued to cross the Atlantic but also the flocks of African blacks deposited by the European slave trade. From the beginning, slavery and later Jim Crow were essential to the American profile. Hence racism became the ugly twin of inequality. Add to this a stupendous influx of Hispanics from Latin America and you have a severely challenged Yankee melting pot.

Third, although the mention of Puritanism may devolve into a very misleading caricature, it is impossible to overlook the prominent role of religion in American life. Throughout its history, and still today, the United States has been a society less secular than Europe. Accordingly, the American constitution insists on the separation of Church and State and explicitly stipulates that the intervention of the federal government shall be limited, not only in matters of religion. This restrictive federalism—implicitly an emphasis on states' rights—was fitting for an expanding nation and has traditionally hindered efforts to establish social reforms on a grand scale.

Finally, perhaps less obvious but not less basic, the American political structure has clearly departed from the European norm by fostering a two-party system. After the early nineteenth century multipartism has rarely succeeded in the USA, and the fate of third parties (Theodore Roosevelt and Ross Perot notwithstanding) has generally been dismal. In modern times political competition has invariably been between Democrats and Republicans in electoral contests that have excluded meaningful participation by other parties. Socialism has consequently lacked representation by a political formation that had a serious chance to influence positively the course of welfare reform. Instead, leftist efforts to overcome resistance to actions of a centralized state in promoting health care have usually done little more than raise irate negative cries against the threat of "socialized medicine."

If this brief sketch of these four factors verges on the self-evident, nevertheless they need to be plainly stated at the outset of any examination of the American way. This is not necessarily to ignore some basic similarities with Europe that induced several comparable social problems. The inescapable results of industrialization and urbanization were everywhere the same: poverty, disability, epidemics, workplace accidents, rising life expectancy of the elderly, and the rest. Yet, like Sweden, America was a relative latecomer to coherent national welfare reforms, and there is little to record in that regard for the entire nineteenth century. Nor, as it turned out, did the United States often follow the European lead in the twentieth.

Not until the First World War did the debate over voluntary or compulsory health insurance begin—an argument in which the principles of obligation and universalism, unlike Europe, were decisively lost in the United States. Eventually only the aged (Medicare) and the poor (Medicaid) would gain major federal assistance, inadequately at that. In most instances these initiatives originated with the Progressive movement, which can be compared with European liberalism as a moderate laissez faire philosophy, albeit with a modicum of state regulation. The political term "liberal," it should be added, was completely redefined in the American context as a vague opprobrium for leftist action.

In the early agitation for workers' compensation, child labor laws, industrial safety measures, and anti-trust legislation, the American Socialist Party remained altogether marginal. Its history can virtually be told through the biography of two men. Eugene Debs, the son of immigrant Alsatian parents, began his career as a Democrat when elected to the General Assembly of Indiana in 1884 at the age of twenty-nine. He was a co-founder of the American Railway Union, one of the first of its kind, and was briefly imprisoned for ordering the Pullman strike of 1894. Turning to socialism, he ran as the party's candidate for the American presidency four consecutive times from 1900 to 1912, then again in 1920 while back in prison for his opposition to the United States participation in the First World War. He never received more than 3 to 6 percent of the popular vote. Released at the end of 1921, he died five years later in a TB sanatorium.

His successor, Norman Thomas, outdid Debs by running for the presidency six times. A Princeton graduate and an ordained minister in the Presbyterian Church, he was ordinarily to be seen in a dapper three-piece suit, scarcely fitting the description of a socialist radical. Like Debs, he criticized the US entry into the First World War, espoused pacifism, and was a conscientious objector. Although the American Socialist Party's platform was formally Marxist, Thomas followed Debs in rejecting revolutionary doctrine. His first nomination for the presidency came in 1928, and he dominated the party thereafter. In the late 1930s he flirted with the idea of a Léon

Blum-like Popular Front, but internal conflicts with communists soon led him to a rabid anti-communist stance. Meanwhile the party went nowhere. In the Second World War Thomas championed the America First movement against participation—until Pearl Harbor, whereupon he fell silent. His last great cause was against the war in Vietnam. He died in 1968 at age eighty-four, and the American Socialist Party has hardly been heard from since. His life again confirmed the obvious moral of the story that the United States has had little room for a third party.

By no means, however, was an active trade union movement excluded. During the interwar years both the CIO and the AFL gained considerable importance as national representatives of organized labor. At first neither appeared as a reliable ally of welfare reform. Especially outspoken against government intervention in such matters was AFL leader Samuel Gompers, although his successor, William Green, did come around after 1933 to support New Deal measures in favor of social security. Throughout, American trade unions had their peculiarities. They stressed voluntarism, employment-based insurance programs, and emphasis on benefits for male industrial workers, with little regard for women. Furthermore, they put no stock in socialism as a political entity. In the melee of the 1930s the result was, whether the unions intended it or not, that large private insurance companies thrived. Prudential, Equitable, and Metropolitan became household names and powerful lobbies. True to form, they also opposed any hint of a compulsory or universalist health and welfare system.

Another organization merits a mention here: the American Medical Association. AMA leaders were initially somewhat divided, since many of them were frank admirers of European reforms. But others continued the longstanding tradition of most medical personnel by castigating state-sponsored schemes as radical, either too Bolshevist or unduly Germanic, not much of a recommendation in the 1930s. Unsurprisingly, the detractors prevailed, and the urge for compulsory insurance legislation grew faint when confronted with the holy alliance of employers, insurers, and physicians.

It is possible now to back up a bit and consider the American case under a different optic, namely the mixed efforts of successive political regimes to steer the course of social reform. Surely the place to start is the advent of Franklin D. Roosevelt's long presidency in the wake of the Great Depression. In retrospect, the initial thrust of the New Deal promised by FDR appears to have been a series of stopgap measures to ease the plight of 12 million unemployed citizens. That description fits a number of government agencies created right after the presidential inauguration of 1933, among them the National Industrial Recovery Act (NIRA) that imposed some industrial regulations, a minimum wage, and collective bargaining rights; the Civilian Conservation Corps (CCC) that provided outdoor jobs for over 2 million workers; and most importantly the Works Progress Administration (WPA) that occupied 8 million more in repairing hospitals, schools, bridges, and roads. But Roosevelt's concern for the longer run was also evident in the passage of a social security plan in 1935, which included old-age pensions, accident insurance, disability assistance, and aid to indigent mothers and children. These enactments had only modest success in restoring a sputtering economy—until the Second World War brought a spectacular industrial boom that made the United States a dominant world economic power.

Nonetheless, one essential element of any future welfare state was conspicuously lacking: a national health insurance program. As previously noted, this potentially game-changing innovation was thwarted by vigorous opposition from employers, private insurance companies, and the AMA. The result was to swell the ranks of private insurance clients, especially through employer-sponsored group plans without direct state participation, meaning Blue Cross, Blue Shield, Kaiser Permanente, and the like. By 1945 over 30 million persons were covered by such organizations, at least half of them by Blue Cross alone. The outcome, in sum, was that the subsequent government-sponsored schemes of Medicare and Medicaid were to become supplementary to private insurance rather than vice versa.

Upon his death FDR was widely acclaimed as a great wartime leader but somewhat more faintly as a social reformer. His successor, Harry S. Truman, attempted to inspire a more vigorous national health insurance system, but to no avail at a time when such initiatives could all too easily be dismissed as "socialized medicine" or indeed communism. It was, after all, the era of Stalin—and of Joseph McCarthy. Beyond that, in the second half of the twentieth century the burden of already established procedures weighed heavily against any significant social reform. While the European nations, each in its own fashion, marched toward what could legitimately be called a welfare state, the United States of America demurred. But it could not hide the two primary flaws of a health care arrangement that was not compulsory: elevated costs and huge gaps in coverage for the uninsured.

Following the inertia of the Eisenhower years, John F. Kennedy's presidency was brief and inconclusive, without a change of course. It was his idea to incorporate a form of obligatory health insurance into the existing social security program. With the perennial specter of "socialized medicine" the AMA again resisted, even though Kennedy did receive support from organized labor and some employers. The lingering issue, as always, was how to finance such reform. Without increased taxation and state subsidies, increased social security benefits and employment-based group health insurance might not be reconciled in one national scheme. After Kennedy's assassination Lyndon B. Johnson showed less deference to the AMA while gathering an informal coalition of insurance companies, hospitals, and business leaders. He finally succeeded in pushing through Medicare and Medicaid in the summer of 1965, which was doubtless the greatest achievement in American health care since the New Deal. Yet it still did not basically alter traditional fee-for-service procedures and was thus not inimical to the previous standards of private medical practice. Moreover, Johnson's "Great Society" left millions under the age of sixty-five without coverage—nearly a quarter of the American population— and thereby failed to match the principle of universalism being adopted by western European nations. Costs for health care were in the meantime exploding. In fact they constituted more than 10 percent of American GDP by the 1980s. All of which occurred within the context of structural regression within a nation that was evolving away from a broad manufacturing base and toward a service and information economy in which lost industrial jobs often meant lost health insurance coverage.

It was to meet these deficiencies that Senator Edward Kennedy proposed a single-payer system (not unlike that of Canada) that would be operated by the federal government and would supersede private group insurance plans. In the America of Richard Nixon such a sweeping legislative act had no chance. Instead, Nixon countered with encouragement for prepaid HMOs (health maintenance organizations) similar to the Kaiser model. Passed through Congress in 1973, this measure's implementation proved to be slow and irregular, mainly because of objection to limitations of patients' right to choose their own private physician as well as the AMA's reluctance to accept restrictions on private medical practice in setting individual fees for service. Hence the expansion of HMOs had to await the 1980s and 1990s, a development that was not a fundamental change but a continuation of insurance programs modified only slightly by stricter government regulation of medical billing practices.

And then there was Bill Clinton or, more precisely, Bill and Hillary. Convinced that the time had come by the end of the twentieth century for a thoroughgoing overhaul of American health care, the new President appointed for that purpose a taskforce headed by his spouse. But they, too, were unable to escape the tight grasp of history and its clinging inequities. Correctly assuming that Ted Kennedy's single-payer system was unfeasible because of entrenched private insurance companies and their lobbyists, the Clintons considered that the only option would be an intricate compromise based on programs offered through employers that would also introduce the so-called "individual mandate," that is, an element of compulsion hitherto lacking, which might include the still uncovered population in a national insurance plan. Unable to achieve a consensus for this ambitious proposal, Hillary Clinton's mission was a failure. Furthermore, no solution was found for the increasingly urgent problem of rising costs for medical care and hospital stays. American welfare and health care would therefore remain essentially voluntary, which is to say inadequate, and the only recourse for the uninsured poor in moments of medical desperation would be a trip to the hospital emergency ward, to be sure at taxpayers' expense.

In all of this commotion socialism played little part except as a pejorative epithet. The American Socialist Party was without leverage, and trade union members, over 90 percent of whom were enrolled in one group insurance plan or another, turned against reform. The setback of the Clintons lasted for over a decade. True, a national prescription drug program was enacted under George W. Bush in 2003, but it was grafted onto the existing Medicare structure, and above all it financially benefited pharmaceutical firms and private insurance companies without providing additional sources of funding. The inevitable results were to increase federal spending, to boost the national deficit, and therewith to raise stronger resistance to further reform legislation.

As it entered the twenty-first century the United States displayed a mixture of public and private health care with embarrassing and costly lacunae. Inflation is ever the enemy of welfare, especially since the growing number of the uninsured is irrepressible. As the rickety structure of the American health care system is presently constituted, the government appears unable to stem this gathering tsunami, and employment-related insurance plans do not promise to be an adequate response as the century wears on. At this writing

"Obamacare"—originally a term of condemnation before being adopted by a young new president—represents a last hope to lay the foundation of a transformative welfare system. Politically, financially, and legally, however, Barack Obama's Affordable Health Care Act remains a question mark.

# CONCLUSION

The focus of this book has manifestly been centered on the origins of socialism and social welfare in western Europe and its American offspring. The problem in conceiving such a survey is not so much what to include as what to omit. In reality, the subject is inexhaustible, and vast areas with their socialistic variations have been left out. What, for instance, of New Zealand or South Africa? Cuba or Brazil? Singapore or Japan? Switzerland or Spain? Russia or China? Although they are well beyond the scope of this study, these cases among others ultimately need to be brought under consideration.

Yet the heart of the matter, what is most essential about it, has been outlined here. To put this into perspective, it is possible to compile a chart of when and where different forms of insurance plans as national programs were first introduced by the nations under consideration:

|               | Health | Sickness | Accident | Pensions | Unemployment |
|---------------|--------|----------|----------|----------|--------------|
| Germany       | 1880   | 1883     | 1884     | 1889     | 1927         |
| France        | 1945   | 1930     | 1898     | 1905     | 1905         |
| Britain       | 1948   | 1911     | 1887     | 1908     | 1911         |
| Sweden        | 1962   | 1910     | 1901     | 1913     | 1934         |
| United States | 2010   | —        | 1930     | 1935     | 1935         |

It is noteworthy that social democracy as a political movement has not always proceeded at the same rhythm as welfare reform. Bismarck's initiatives in the 1880s came at a time when the SPD was still weak and isolated; its influence was limited to the vaguely perceived threat of a "red menace" that prodded the new German state into defensive action. In both France and Britain the ebb and flow of party politics undoubtedly had more impact on parliamentary decisions, but the role of liberalism was no less crucial than that of the socialism for the passage of public reforms. Neither the French Socialist Party nor the British Labour Party could claim full credit for the advances realized mostly in the first half of the twentieth century and then confirmed after the Second World War. Even the eventual paragon of Sweden was largely shaped at the outset by coalition governments whose efforts were later superseded by the dominant strain of Scandinavian socialism. As the for the American Socialist Party, it could never make much of a mark within a two-party system in which the Democratic Party from Franklin D. Roosevelt to Barack Obama took a belated lead in promoting social reform.

Nonetheless, since the late nineteenth century socialism has represented and ceaselessly boosted the aspiration of millions of people for a more equitable society. Reviewing this phenomenon nation by nation enables us to grasp basic distinctions among them but also to define their characteristics in common. In other words, we can determine what the concept of socialism means by specifying its fundamental elements. Here they may be reduced to four.

1) *A positive view of the state.* The reformist and centrist nature of socialist doctrine cannot be in doubt. Historically, again and again, the most essential feature of socialistic endeavor has been a compromise: at the same time to modify the capitalist system and to reject any revolutionary impulse to overthrow it. Important as Karl Marx was in formulating the terms for understanding modern industrial society, in no instance—the much later seventy years of the peripheral Soviet Union excepted—did his vision of historical evolution prevail. Instead, revisionism became the heart of the socialist movement in one incarnation after another. This development could only be possible once the Marxist notion was abandoned that the state by definition could only be the instrument of the ruling class. Rather, in the socialist perspective, it was capable of becoming a genuine agent of reform. It was one of America's greatest liberals (by the European definition), Ronald Reagan, who uttered the famous epithet: "Big government is not the solution. It is the problem." Certainly that shibboleth was far from the socialist conviction that the state's responsibility is to curb social inequality by political means within the framework of a traditional parliamentary system. Hence the completely appropriate sobriquet of social democracy.

2) *A redistribution of wealth.* There is no secret about a Robin Hood element within the socialist camp. Marx's assertion that the proper functioning of capitalism requires that a few be fortunate and many wanting remains perfectly valid, and proponents of socialist theory could not well deny it. But they could propose to mitigate the contrasting extremes of riches and poverty. How to do so, however, has long been a complex and contentious issue. Without getting too far into the weeds, the foregoing chapters have attempted to illustrate the vexing problem of financing social reform measures. Bismarck basically adopted a contributory model, that is, a program whereby employers, workers, and the state each provided a share of the funding. For labor this necessarily involved a withholding scheme through some kind of payroll tax. At one time or another, objections were raised to this arrangement in nations where reformers preferred a progressive taxation with rates adjusted from bottom to top according to income. Thereupon appeared controversies about whether compensation, especially when it came to pensions, should be flat-rated for all or determined on a scale of earnings. In several instances universalism was appealing in theory but problematic in practice. Even the most equitable of European societies, Sweden, a movement back to Bismarck was discernible, supported as it was by those—notably trade unionists—who disputed the award of equal benefits to the wealthy as to the needy.

3) *A platform of solidarism.* The term "solidarism" has had several definitions, and in the case of early twentieth-century France it was even applied to a specific political cluster located somewhere between liberalism and socialism. We can be more precise. The solidaristic ethic connoted the universal application of social security to every citizen of a given nation. In the beginning welfare was ordinarily designed to meet the most urgent needs of selected portions of the population: injured industrial workers, indigent families, impoverished farmers, disabled war veterans, widows and orphans. But the solidarist contention was that all citizens should have the right to protection from distress and therewith a guaranteed minimum existence, regardless of their social status or special circumstances. This viewpoint was not necessarily or exclusively socialistic. Indeed, the trade unions sometimes opposed it, because they objected to losing privileges that were awarded under certain original regulations of welfare legislation, such as those of Bismarckian Germany. Yet as time wore on, notably in the second half of the twentieth century, opinion tipped (however grudgingly) in the direction of solidarism, with which social democracy became increasingly identified.

4) *An adoption of the welfare state.* The perfect social system has not been devised. Yet, at whatever pace and by whatever means, the major states of western Europe have arrived at some version of the welfare state. Throughout, socialism has been indispensable to this evolution, even when its political

party representation was not always dominant—as in Bismarck's Germany, De Gaulle's France, or Lloyd George's Britain. The direct socialist impact on reform in Europe was perhaps least in Germany, most in Tage Erlander's Sweden. Time and again, the intention of socialists proved not to be incompatible with capitalism, although they steadfastly sought to moderate it. At the risk of undue repetition, there is only one conclusion to be drawn from this repeated pattern: that western European socialism has forged an immutable and laudable character of reformism and centrism dedicated to a more equitable society.

Yet what of the United States? Statistical projections are questionable, but it seems that nearly 50 million Americans— that is, almost one citizen in five—still have no health insurance whatever, and the number of uninsured may be growing. Surely that disturbing fact is shameful, scandalous, unworthy of a great nation in comparison with western Europe. It appears that a decisive step toward correction of these social ills was taken by the decision of the United States Supreme Court in June 2012 to allow the individual mandate of the Affordable Care Act to stand—even though that opinion was justified on the narrow and dubious grounds that compulsory health insurance was in effect a form of taxation permissible under the Constitution. Still, this verdict must be seen as a victory for the Obama administration because it will allow the implementation of more health care provisions in the Act, several of which are very popular and are likely to gain increasing political support as they come on line. The ultimate result nonetheless remains in doubt. Will the United States follow one or another of the European examples? If so, there is an argument to be made that Barack Obama should be pleased to be called a socialist and to be accused of leading America to a welfare state. After all, if this work has demonstrated anything, it is that the charge of "radical socialism" is oxymoronic.

# INDEX

Affordable Health Care Act, 66, 72

AFL (American Federation of Labor), 60

Africa, 57

agriculture, 8, 14, 31, 38, 49, 51, 53, 71

Alsace-Lorraine, 33, 59

American Medical Association (AMA), 60-64

American Railway Union, 59

American Socialist Party, 59-60, 65, 68

Amsterdam, 29

anti-Semitism, 19

anti-socialist laws, 11, 14

Armistice of 1918, 17

Assistance Médicale Gratuite, 30

Attlee, Clement, 46-47

Austria, 16

Bavaria, 16-18

Bebel, August, 10-11, 14

Berlin, 2, 11, 17-18, 23, 36

Bernstein, Eduard, 14, 51

Beveridge, William, 46-47

Bevan, Aneurin, 46

Bevin, Ernest, 47

Bismarck, Otto von, 9-13, 19, 22, 24, 28, 42, 50, 52-53, 68, 70-72

Blanc, Louis, 26

Blue Cross, 62

Blue Shield, 62

Blum, Léon, 35, 59-60

Bolshevism, 4, 17, 32, 61

Bonaparte, Napoleon, 1, 7

Bonn Republic, 22

Borsig, 8

Bourgeois, Léon, 30

bourgeoisie, 3, 28

Brandt, Willy, 22

Branting, Hjalmar, 51

Brazil, 67

Breslau, 7

Britain, 1, 4, 38, 41-48, 52-53, 68, 72

British Medical Association, 47

Brüning, Heinrich, 20

Bundesrepublik. See Bonn Republic

bureaux de bienfaisance, 27, 31

Bush, George W., 65

Cabet, Étienne, 26

Caisse Nationale de Sécurité Sociale, 37

Caisse Nationale des Retraites, 30

Canada, 64
capitalism, 3-6, 13-14, 21, 23, 30, 34, 40, 48, 69-70, 72
Catholic Church, 18, 25, 27, 31
Chamber of Deputies (France), 34, 38
charity, 9, 27, 30-31
children, 14, 16, 21, 27, 30, 42, 54-55, 59, 61
China, 67
Chirac, Jacques, 39
Churchill, Winston S., 44, 46
Civilian Conservation Corps (CCC), 61
Clinton, Bill, 64-65
Clinton, Hillary, 64-65
Cologne, 7
commerce, 1, 9, 37, 41
communism, 13, 19, 35, 60, 62
Communist Party of Germany (KPD), 15-18
compulsory system, 12-13, 25, 30-33, 36-38, 44, 53, 58, 60-61, 63-64, 72
Confédération Générale du Travail (CGT), 37
Congress of Industrial Unions (CIO), 60
Conseil Supérieur de l'Assistance Publique, 30
conservatism, 18, 43, 45, 51
contributory system, 31, 38-39, 44-45, 50-51, 70
Couverture Médicale Universelle (CMU), 39
Cuba, 67

Daladier, Edouard, 35
Debs, Eugene, 59
Democratic Party (USA), 58-59, 68

demography, 1, 8, 26, 32, 41
Denmark, 52-53
Deutsche Arbeitsfront (DAF), 20
Dreyfus Affair, 28

Ebert, Friedrich, 17
École Normale Supérieure, 29
economy, 4, 8, 10, 12, 14, 19-21, 24, 35-36, 47, 61-63
eighteenth century, 8, 41
Eisenach, 10
Eisenhower, Dwight D., 63
Eisner, Kurt, 18-19
Elberfeld, 9
Engels, Friedrich, 3
Erlander, Tage, 52, 72
Europe, 1, 5-6, 8, 11-13, 19, 28, 36, 41, 52, 56-58, 61-63, 67, 69-73

Fabian Society, 43, 46
factories, 1, 8-9, 12, 15, 42
family assistance, 12, 32, 38, 57
farmers. See agriculture, peasants
fascism, 20. See also National Socialism
federalism, 57
fee-for-service billing, 22, 54, 63-64
Fifth Republic (France), 38
finance, 31, 34, 44-45, 50, 55, 63
Finland, 53
First World War, 4-5, 13, 15-17, 25, 31-33, 44-46, 58-59
flat-rate premiums, 44-45, 47, 53, 55, 70
Fourier, Charles, 26
Fourth Republic (France), 36-38
France, 1, 10, 24-40, 44, 46, 53, 68, 71-72
Frederick the Great, 8

French Communist Party (PCF), 35, 38
French Revolution, 28

Gaulle, Charles de, 36, 38, 72
General German Workers' Association, 9-10
German Democratic Republic (DDR), 21-22
Germany, 1, 3-4, 7-26, 28-35, 42, 44, 46-48, 50-53, 61, 68, 71-72
Giscard d'Estaing, Valérie, 38
Goethe, Johann Wolfgang von, 56
Gompers, Samuel, 60
Göring, Hermann, 20
Great Depression, 19, 45, 61
Green, William, 60
Groener, Wilhelm, 17
Guesde, Jules, 28-29, 32

Hamburg, 11
Hardie, Keir, 43
Health Maintenance Organizations (HMOs), 64
Hegel, Georg Wilhelm Friedrich, 2-3, 5
Hitler, Adolf, 18-20
Holland, 16
hospitals, 13, 22, 32-33, 36, 38, 47, 61, 63, 65

Independent Labour Party (Britain), 43
Independent Social Democratic Party of Germany (USPD), 15, 18
indigence. *See* poverty
individual mandate, 31, 37, 64. *See also* compulsory system

industrialization, 9, 24, 34, 41, 49, 53, 58, 62, 69
industrial revolution, 1, 7
industry, 1, 3-4, 8, 12-13, 15, 34, 37-38, 40, 42, 49, 52, 60, 63
inflation of 1923, 19
insurance. *See* social insurance
insurance companies, 33, 42, 60, 62-65

Japan, 67
Jaurès, Jean, 29-30, 35
Jews, 18
Johnson, Lyndon B., 63

Kaiser Permanente, 62, 64
Kaiserreich, 8, 10-11, 13-14, 17, 19
Kant, Immanuel, 18
Kautsky, Karl, 14
Kennedy, Edward ("Ted"), 64
Kennedy, John F., 63
Keynes, John Maynard, 48
Krupp, 8

Labour Party, 43-47, 68
Laroque, Pierre, 36-37
Lassalle, Ferdinand, 9-10
Latin America, 57
Lenin, Nikolai, 4, 17
Leviné, Eugen, 18-19
Ley, Robert, 20
liberalism, 9, 11-12, 24-25, 27-30, 34, 37, 43-46, 48-51, 58-59, 68, 71
Liebknecht, Karl, 14, 17
Liebknecht, Wilhelm, 10, 14
Lloyd George, David, 44, 72
London, 3-4, 36-37, 42, 46
Ludwig III (Bavaria), 16
Luxemburg, 1
Luxemburg, Rosa, 14, 17

manufacturing. *See* industry
Marxism, 14, 18, 51, 59
Marx, Karl, 1-7, 21, 26, 28, 48, 69-70
maternity care, 22, 26, 30, 33, 54
Matignon accords, 35
McCarthy, Joseph, 62
McDonald, Ramsay, 45
medical care. *See* physicians
Medicaid, 58, 62-63
Medicare, 58, 62-63, 65
Millerand, Alexandre, 28
ministerialism, 28
Mitterand, François, 39
Monod, Henri, 30
Moselle River, 1
Munich, 18, 35
mutualism, 27, 29, 31-33, 37, 42-44

natalism, 26, 32
National Health Service (NHS), 37, 46-47
National Industrial Recovery Act (NIRA), 61
National Insurance Act (NIA), 44-45
nationalism, 5, 16, 20, 29, 31-32
National Liberal Party (Germany), 12
National Socialism, 18-20, 22, 35
New Deal, 60, 63
New Zealand, 67
nineteenth century, 4-5, 7-8, 24-27, 36, 41, 49-50, 52, 57-58, 68
Nixon, Richard, 64
North German Confederation, 10
Norway, 53
notability, 27, 31

Obama, Barack, 66, 68, 72-73

obligation. *See* compulsory system
Old Age Pension Act (Britain), 43
Old Age Pensions Commission (Sweden), 50
orphans, 14, 45, 71
Orwell, George, 43

pacifism, 29, 35, 59
Palme, Olaf, 52
Papen, Franz von, 20
Paris, 27, 29, 36
Paris Commune, 4, 10-11, 28
*patronat,* 25, 29, 31
Pearl Harbor, 60
peasants, 15, 17. *See also* agriculture
pensions. *See* social insurance
Perot, Ross, 57
Pétain, Philippe, 36
physicians, 33, 37-38, 47, 51, 55, 61, 63-64
Poincaré, Raymond, 31
Pompidou, Georges, 38
poor laws, 9, 42-43
Popular Front, 35, 60
Potsdam conference, 21
poverty, 5, 8-9, 26, 30, 41, 45, 48, 52, 54, 58, 61, 70-71
Presbyterian Church, 59
Princeton University, 59
Progressivism (USA), 58
proletariat. *See* working class
Proudhon, Pierre-Joseph, 26
Prussia, 7-10, 28, 52
public assistance. *See* social reform
Puritanism, 57

racism, 57
Radical Party (France), 28, 34-35
railways, 8, 42, 47
Reagan, Ronald, 69

reform. *See* social reform
Reichstag, 11, 13, 16
religion, 57. *See also* Catholic
   Church, Presbyterian Church
Republican Party (USA), 58
revisionism, 14-15, 25, 29, 51, 69
revolution, 4-5, 14, 25, 59, 69;
   of 1848, 3-4, 9, 26; of 1917
   (Russia), 4; of 1918 (Germany),
   16-17
revolutionary councils, 17
Reynaud, Paul, 35
Rhineland, 7
Rome, 1, 43
Roosevelt, Franklin D., 61-62, 68
Roosevelt, Theodore, 57
Rosenheim, 18
rural population. *See* agriculture
Russia, 18, 67, 69

Saint-Simon, Henri de, 26
Saltsjöbaden Agreement, 51
sanatoriums, 13, 44, 59
Saxony, 10-11
Scandinavia, 53, 68. *See also*
   Denmark, Finland, Norway,
   Sweden
Schmidt, Helmut, 22
Second World War, 31, 35, 45-46,
   52, 60-61, 68
Section Française de l'Internationale
   Ouvrière (SFIO), 29, 31,
   34-35, 37-38, 68
Shaw, George Bernard, 43
Siemens, 8
Silesia, 7
Singapore, 67
single-payer system, 64
social democracy, 6, 10-11, 13,
   15-17, 19, 21, 23-31, 33-36,
   39, 48, 51, 65, 67-68, 73

Social Democratic Party of
   Germany (SPD), 10-11, 13,
   15-17, 19-21, 68
Social Democratic Party of Sweden,
   49-50, 52
social inequality, 5, 48, 57
social insurance, 12-14, 21, 32-34,
   36-39, 42, 44-45, 50, 52-53,
   58, 60, 63-64, 68; accident,
   12, 14-15, 27, 42, 45, 61,
   6871; disability, 12, 15, 27,
   33, 44, 54, 61, 68; old-age
   pensions, 12, 22, 27, 30, 33,
   43, 45, 50, 52, 55, 61, 68, 70;
   illness, 12, 15, 22, 27, 33, 44,
   54, 68; unemployment, 19,
   38, 44, 68
socialization, 19
social legislation, 9, 12-13, 19-21,
   26-27, 30-31, 33, 36-37, 39,
   41-42, 45, 48, 50, 55-56, 59,
   61, 64, 71
social reform, 8, 11, 13-14, 16,
   19-22, 26-27, 30-34, 36-37,
   39, 42-45, 47, 49-50, 52, 57,
   60-65, 68-70
social security, 13-15, 20-21, 23,
   25, 36-39, 46, 60-61, 63, 71
soldiers, 15, 17, 19, 32, 45, 71
solidarism, 30, 33, 71
South Africa, 67
Soviet Union. *See* Russia
Spain, 67
Spartacus League, 15, 17
Stalin, Joseph, 62
Stockholm, 52
strikes, 10, 13, 25, 31, 51, 59
Sweden, 22, 38, 49-55, 68, 70, 72
Swedish Central Bank, 51
Switzerland, 67
syndicalism, 25, 29

taxation, 13, 21, 27, 31-32, 38-39, 44, 46, 50-54, 63, 70, 72
technology, 1, 13
Third International, 35
Third Republic (France), 28, 31-32, 36
Thomas, Norman, 59-60
Tours congress, 34
trade unions, 9-11, 14, 16-17, 20-21, 25, 29, 31, 34-37, 40, 42-43, 45, 47, 51, 53, 60, 65, 70-71. *See also* syndicalism
transportation, 2, 8, 13. *See also* railways
Trier (Trèves), 1
Truman, Harry S., 62
tuberculosis, 13, 16, 27, 44, 59. *See also* sanatoriums
twentieth century, 27, 43, 58, 62, 64, 68, 71
twenty-first century, 39, 65

unemployment, 8, 15, 19-20, 32, 42, 45, 51, 54, 61
Unemployment Workmen Act, 43
*union sacrée*, 29, 32
United Kingdom. *See* Britain
United States of America, 6, 56-69, 72-73
universalism, 16, 19, 22, 36-38, 44, 49-50, 52-53, 55, 58, 60, 63, 70-71
Ural Mountains, 56
urbanization, 8, 15, 26, 49-50, 53, 58

Versailles, 10, 33
veterans. *See* soldiers
Vichy, 35-37
Vienna, 7
Vietnam War, 60
voluntarism, 10-12, 27, 32, 37, 42, 58, 65

wages, 30, 35, 40, 70
Wales, 46
War of 1870, 7, 10
Waterloo, 7
Webb, Beatrice, 43, 46
Webb, Sidney, 43, 46
Weimar Republic, 16-17, 19-20, 22
welfare state, 15-16, 22-24, 30, 32-33, 36, 39, 43, 46-47, 52-55, 62, 65-67, 71-73
widows, 14, 45, 71
Wilhelm I (Kaiser), 11
Wilhelm II (Kaiser), 16-17
Wittelsbach dynasty, 17. *See also* Ludwig III
women, 14, 16, 21-22, 27, 42, 55, 60-61. *See also* maternity care, widows
working class, 2-6, 9-12, 14-15, 17, 20, 27, 29, 34-38, 40, 43-44, 48-50, 52, 60, 70-71
working hours, 14, 19 34-35, 42
Workmen's Compensation Act, 42
Works Progress Administration (WPA), 61

Zurich, 14

www.ingramcontent.com/pod-product-compliance
Lightning Source LLC
Chambersburg PA
CBHW031302280526
45784CB00004B/1953